eBay for Beginners

Other Books of Interest

BP600 The Internet for the Older Generation

BP601 Computing for the Older Generation

BP602 Digital Photography and Computing for the Older Generation

PB514 Windows XP Explained

BP538 Windows XP for Beginners

Acknowledgements

The author and publishers would like to thank the following for their help in the preparation of this book:

My students

Jim Gatenby

Harry Speed

Tallulah Speed

Sheila Nixon

Especially John Bussey for the many hours of nuts and bolts assistance.

eBay for Beginners

Cherry Nixon

BERNARD BABANI (publishing) Ltd
The Grampians
Shepherds Bush Road
London W6 7NF
England

www.babanibooks.com

Please Note

Although every care has been taken with the production of this book to ensure that the information contained herewith is correct, the publishers and author do not accept responsibility for any matters arising from its use. From time to time there may be changes to the eBay site and users must take account of this. There may also be changes of policy and alteration in fees and fee structure. The views expressed are those of the author and may be at variance with the ideas of others. Where step by step instructions have been given they are based on Windows XP.

First Published – September 2004

Reprinted – December 2004

Reprinted – April 2005

Revised and Reprinted – September 2006

British Library Cataloguing in Publication Data.

A catalogue record for this book is available from the British Library.

ISBN 0 85934 551 3

Cover Design by Gregor Arthur

Printed and bound in Great Britain by Cox & Wyman Ltd, Reading, Berks

About this Book

This book is a beginner's guide to eBay.co.uk. It is designed to show novices and new users how to start trading on the UK site and easy ways to avoid the problems and pitfalls that can befall the inexperienced. It is not a definitive work on eBay and there are many aspects of this site that have been left out in order to present a simple route to basic buying and selling. It is recommended that this book is initially read in its entirety, however, key information is repeated to enable its use as an easy reference work. This book is more than just a guide and offers a structure of organization and mindset for long-term successful trading. Above all else it is a simple approach that allows technologically untalented people to experience the joys of this amazing site.

Trademarks

eBay.co.uk, eBay.com and PayPal, are trademarks or registered trademarks of their respective companies.

All other trademarks are the registered and legally protected trademarks of the companies who make the products. There is no intent to use the trademark generically moreover; readers should investigate ownership of a trademark before using it for any purpose.

About the Author

Cherry Nixon (BA) is a trained teacher (PGCE) and experienced eBay tutor. She created this country's first hands-on course to teach people how to trade on eBay.co.uk. The idea came from her first course, 'Learn About Antiques & Collectables'. It was through her antiques and collectables teaching activities that she came across eBay and was so delighted with the site that she urged her students to embrace it for their buying and selling. However she soon became aware of a climate of reticence and realized that whilst the majority of her students were very keen to use eBay they needed her to show them how. Confident that she had found a gap in the market she set about creating a step-by-step course 'Buying and Selling on eBay for Technological Simpletons'. This ground-breaking course has been enormously popular, drawing a wide variety of students with diverse motivations but all of whom are keen to get started on eBay. Amongst her students are: specialist collectors, business people looking to expand their selling activities, disillusioned individuals who want to become self-employed, people with mobility problems, pensioners who want to supplement their incomes and people who have inherited houses full of things that they want to sell in the most cost-effective manner. Some older people have admitted attending the course in order to be able to join in the conversations! Presenting her eBay course has given her a unique understanding of what people require to get started on eBay and this book mirrors her classes.

Contents

1. A New Concept

Trading Ideas

Imagine a scenario where society developed on a very different path and the only means of buying was online. Food, drink, household appliances, clothes, books, CD's, in fact every single item was purchased via the internet in auctions and stores. These goods were gathered up from vast warehouses and delivered to the customer's door. There was simply no other way to buy things.

One day a bright young trainee executive, called Aaron, woke up with an idea. It was a radical new concept for buying and selling and he felt sure it was a winner. He hurried along to his boss's office and knocked boldly on the door. An authoritative voice invited him to enter and Aaron burst into the sumptuous state-of-the-art office and strode up to the large desk. Behind it sat Rhoda, the dynamic new head of enterprises, who had recently been awarded the title 'Idea Spotter of the Year'. She raised one eyebrow to signal her readiness for his message.

'I've got a new idea that I think might change the way we do things. In fact it could change the whole of society', Aaron began enthusiastically.

'What's that then', she enquired. Her voice was flat but her eyebrow remained interested.

'It's about the way we buy things', he continued.

'And that is...?' She spoke sharply. Time is money and Rhoda had none to waste.

'My idea is sheds. Proper, actual sheds where people do their shopping. We could call them shops', he said pertly.

'What do you mean ...shops?' She enquired, intrigued.

'Well, I thought it would be a great idea to have buildings that contain merchandise where people could visit and browse to make their selections'.

Rhoda looked puzzled. 'I don't get it, how would that work?'

Aaron opened his mouth to reply when Rhoda continued. 'You mean that people would get into their cars and join queues of traffic to reach the sheds with the merchandise. Then they would drive round and round in the hope of finding somewhere to leave their car, parting with a significant sum of money to do so. Then they would traipse to the shops where they would have to fight their way through crowds to find what they want to buy. It goes without saying they would have to queue to pay. Then they would stagger back to their car, providing they could remember where they left it, and then make their way home through the driving rain'.

As she finished speaking she looked back at Aaron.

'Forget it', he agreed sheepishly, 'it was a crazy idea'.

The Wonder of Online Trading

Online Trading has arrived and if we can only embrace and master it there are many advantages. You can select items in the comfort of your home, saving the time and cost of the journey. Online commerce allows people with restricted mobility the opportunity to purchase from a wide range of products and without any special arrangements. It offers countless people greater independence and a richer life.

The Magic of eBay's Online Auctions

eBay's online auctions, the original format offered and subject of this guide, represent a specific type of online buying experience and lie at the most exciting end of the consumer spectrum. They combine the heart-stopping excitement of an auction with the immediacy of the internet and the reach of a global market. They offer everyone who has access to the internet the opportunity to take advantage of this unprecedented market. There need be no middle people involved as you reach your buyer and seller direct. Typically prices start low and buyers are lured by the possibility of a snip. eBay auctions appeal to the bargain hunter and gambler in all of us. Buyers reap the benefit of a vast supply of goods, new and old, whilst sellers locate their perfect market. eBay auctions have unearthed forgotten items that have astounded and delighted enthusiasts. Every serious collector needs to include eBay's auctions into their portfolio of buying activities and many consider it their primary source. It is an idiosyncratic form of buying and selling that has revolutionized consumerism and hit the spot for millions of traders. eBay has changed the commercial world.

Overview of an eBay auction

- The seller selects an item to enter into auction.
- The seller takes suitable pictures to attract bidders and show the item.
- The seller chooses the most appropriate category in which to list the item.
- The seller selects a title incorporating key words.
- The seller describes the item carefully, including damage and flaws as well as the positive aspects.
- The seller selects a time span for the auction to run.
- The seller decides the opening price, below which bids are not accepted.
- The seller may decide to start the item off at a very low price to tempt the buyers.
- The seller may opt for a reserve price (£50 +).
- Interested parties place bids during the auction.
- When the time is up, the auction ends and no more bids are accepted.
- The high bidder wins the item and receives an email from eBay confirming the final price.
- The buyer and seller make contact to agree a total price to include P& P. (Buyers pay shipping).
- Buyer sends payment.
- Seller receives and clears payment.
- Seller carefully packs and sends goods.
- Buyer receives item and checks it carefully.
- Buyer and seller leave Feedback rating and comment.

What You Can / Cannot Sell

It is often said that you can buy and sell anything on eBay, but in practice there are restrictions. The site is policed by the eBay team but most of the information regarding illegal listings comes from eBay users themselves. eBay act immediately to stop these auctions. The limitations are entirely sensible, for example you cannot sell illegal or dangerous items. Some of the prohibited items are listed below but for a complete overview of the policy you should go to **Prohibited, Questionable and Infringing Items** in **Site Map**.

Examples of Items Not Allowed

Aeroplane Tickets

Alcohol

Animals

Animal Products – some things are prohibited

Counterfeit Currency

Credit Cards

Drugs and Drug Equipment

Eurostar Tickets

Firearms and Ammunition

Human Parts and Remains

Lockpicking Devices

Lottery Tickets

Mailing Lists and Personal Information

Prescription Drugs

Shares and Securities

1 A New Concept

2. History of eBay

The Creation of eBay

eBay, the online auction site, was launched in the summer of 1995. Far from being the inspired creation of a dollar hungry capitalist it was originally established as a free service for collectors. It is amazing to consider that the online site that has a global turnover of billions of dollars per annum was launched on a shoe-string with a minuscule marketing budget. The success that followed took everyone by surprise, including its founder, Pierre Omidyar.

Pierre Omidyar

Pierre Omidyar was born in Paris in 1967 to French Iranian parents who had been sent to France in the 1960s to gain a better education than was on offer at the time in their home country. Pierre's father studied medicine and his mother was a linguist. In 1973 the Omidyar family moved to the USA where Pierre continued his education. From the outset Pierre was drawn to computers, a field in which he naturally excelled. He was the kind of boy who wrote computer programs for fun and he would sneak off to teach himself to program in BASIC. It was no surprise when he decided to study computer science at university or that his first job was as a Macintosh programmer.

Enter the Internet

The 1980s was an exciting time for a young talented computer buff and Pierre moved around between different companies – Innovative Data Design, Claris, eShop – as opportunities came his way. However, it was his job with General Magic that gave him exposure to the internet, the latest thrill for the computer crowd and for whom the excitement was about to escalate.

Making the Internet Accessible

The invention of the World Wide Web in 1990 transformed the internet into a creative opportunists dream. This new Internet enabled anyone with a PC and modem to reach documents stored on its computers and had the potential to connect everyone in the world. The possibilities seemed limitless. Dial-up service providers were bringing millions of Americans online and internet entrepreneurs went in frantic search of commercial opportunities. New creatures called internet investors were throwing money at online entrepreneurs with an even half-credible idea, and it was as ventures were springing up like daisies in a field that Pierre sat down to create a program for an auction site. It was called AuctionWeb, later known as eBay, and was destined to change the commercial world.

Combining the Internet and the Auction

Pierre had never attended an auction himself but was attracted to the idea of a mechanism whereby price was set by market forces. There were many fixed price online stores but Pierre liked the idea of a site which gave a starting price and allowed people to bid. He considered that this would create 'the perfect market' in which interested parties could fight it out.

Knocking Out the Program

One Friday afternoon he made a start on his new program and by Labor Day in the summer of 1995 it was complete. The initial site, with its black-blue text against a grey background, was as dull as the concept was exciting. The original program only allowed users to do three things: view items, list items and place bids. He realized that he would have to offer a framework for selling and he created general headings like, books, comics, collectables, computer hardware, consumer electronics, etc.

Free For Collectors

Pierre established AuctionWeb as a free service for collectors and from the outset he was under pressure to keep his costs down. He wrote the program as cheaply as he could by pulling in freeware from the internet and operated the site from home. He used the service provider Best with whom he already had a £30 dollar a month account and to keep his outgoings to an absolute minimum he added AuctionWeb to his existing website. He had previously formed a company called Echo Bay Technology, a fictional name that was chosen because it sounded good. In a roundabout way it is through this that eBay got its name.

Stumbling Across a Name

Pierre needed to select a name but when he tried to register EchoBay.com he discovered that this had already been snapped by a Canadian gold mining company. Pierre shrugged it off and came up with an alternative – eBay.com.

eBay.co.uk

eBay.co.uk, our site and the subject of this book, was founded in October 1999. Since then growth has been rapid and by January 2006 eBay.co.uk had 11.5 million registered users. More significantly research showed that over a third of active Internet users within a given month visited this site. In a few short years eBay.co.uk has become the UK's number one e-commerce site with over three million items for sale at any one time in over 13,000 categories.

Brief Summary of Trading Activity on eBay.co.uk

During a Typical Day on eBay.co.uk someone buys:

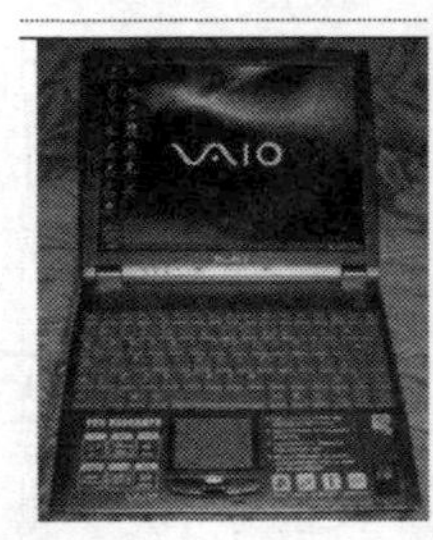

A woman's handbag every 36 seconds
A car every 2 minutes
A toy car every 26 seconds
A laptop every 2 minutes
A mobile phone every 21 seconds

The Advantages of Trading on eBay

This high level of activity is good news for eBay traders and means that they have a vast choice of items to buy and an enormous potential market for the things they wish to sell. eBay do not charge buyers and the fees for selling items in online auctions represent excellent value for money when considering the size of the market and compared with other methods.

The Advantages of Using eBay.co.uk

It makes sense for British people to use the UK site, as:

- Auctions are primarily conducted in pounds sterling and the onus is on all buyers, based here and abroad, to make sterling payments.
- Buyers and sellers can choose whether to trade globally or merely within this country. This is helpful for new traders who want their first transactions to be home-based where they are familiar with the currency and postal costs. It is also useful when buying modest items whose cost of shipping from abroad would be inappropriate. The ability to trade within this country is also helpful when buying items that would be expensive to ship from abroad. Some items, like cars with right-hand drive, are specific to this country and are best sold within our shores.
- The other advantage of the UK site is that instructions on the site contain English rather than American expressions and phrases.

The headquarters for eBay.co.uk is in Richmond, Surrey, just south west of London.

Myths Dispelled -16 Basic Facts About eBay

1. To trade on eBay you require access to the internet and an email address.

2. eBay facilitates contact between buyers and sellers but does not usually become involved in the transaction.

3. The details of transactions are organized by the traders.

4. Buyers pay sellers direct - payment does not pass via eBay.

5. Sellers send the items direct to the buyer, they are not held by eBay.

6. You have to be over 18 years old to buy or sell on eBay.

7. Before you buy or sell on eBay you need to register.

8. To register as a buyer you need to enter your details and email address.

9. To register as a seller you need a debit or credit card.

10. eBay do not charge buyers but most sellers request buyers pay postage and packing

11. eBay charge sellers a small fee which consists of an insertion fee and a final value fee.

12. The insertion fee is non-returnable but the final value fee only applies when the item sells.

13. Both parties are invited to post feedback, a short report about the transaction and rating.

14. eBay has a preferred online payment system, PayPal.

15. PayPal is free to buyers though sellers are charged a small fee.

16. eBay is a trading community whose members police and safeguard the site.

3. Introduction to the Site

Locating the Site

Log onto the internet and when the opening page comes up type www.ebay.co.uk into the web browser.

The eBay home page, as shown below, will appear.

Highlights of the Home Page

Calling up eBay's home page is rather like walking into the entrance hall of a large and impressive business. There are lots of different 'doors' known as links and each is clearly labelled with what you will find inside. This makes undertaking different tasks on eBay very straightforward.

Categories

On the left-hand side of the home page is a list of categories commencing with Antiques & Art, Automotive, Books, Comics & Magazines, etc. They are listed in alphabetical order. At any one time there are millions of items for sale in eBay auctions and they are entered into categories by their sellers.

As eBay trading expands and categories become vast they are broken down into **sub-categories**. There are now thousands of sub-categories and they enable buyers to 'window shop' and browse for things.

Home Page Links

Situated along the top of the home page, as shown below, are different links that enable you to perform various activities. They are all useful but you have to bear in mind that some duplicate what is on offer.

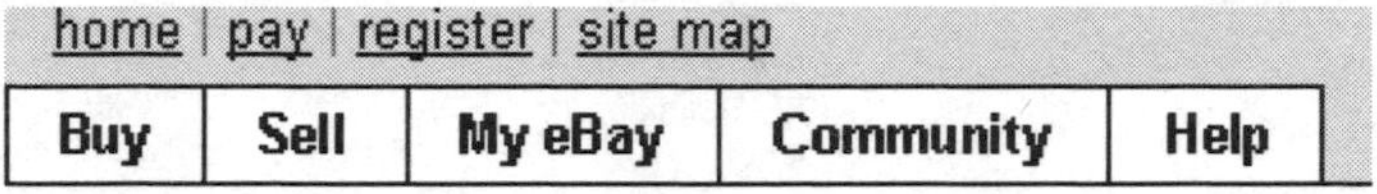

home | pay | register | site map

Buy	Sell	My eBay	Community	Help

At the very top are:

Home – this is where you are currently situated and where you can easily return by clicking on this link at the top of any page.

Pay – initiates payment.

Register – brings up the form for registering. You will need to register to buy and sell on eBay.

Site map – lists everything you will find on the site. It is probably the most useful page for a new user and you should take some time to familiarize yourself with it. It contains a direct link to everything the site contains and when you are up-and-running and need to perform a specific task, it is a good place to go to make a start. When you are confident with the basics of buying and selling you may want to have a further look at site map to see what else is on offer. The next few pages gives a taste of what is available in Site Map but it only scratches the surface!

Site Map is arranged under five main headings:

Buy, Sell, My eBay, Community and Help.

Site Map

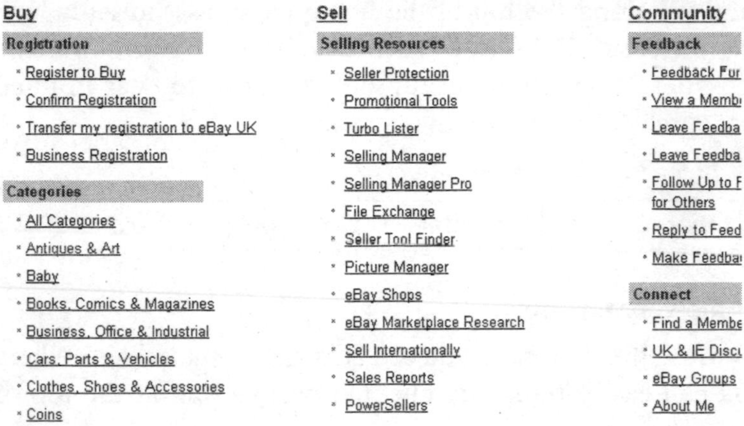

Buy

Registration

- Register to Buy
- Confirm Registration
- Transfer my registration to eBay UK
- Business Registration

Categories

- All Categories
- Antiques & Art
- Baby
- Books, Comics & Magazines
- Business, Office & Industrial
- Cars, Parts & Vehicles
- Clothes, Shoes & Accessories
- Coins

Sell

Selling Resources

- Seller Protection
- Promotional Tools
- Turbo Lister
- Selling Manager
- Selling Manager Pro
- File Exchange
- Seller Tool Finder
- Picture Manager
- eBay Shops
- eBay Marketplace Research
- Sell Internationally
- Sales Reports
- PowerSellers

Community

Feedback

- Feedback Fur
- View a Memb
- Leave Feedba
- Leave Feedba
- Follow Up to F for Others
- Reply to Feed
- Make Feedba

Connect

- Find a Membe
- UK & IE Discu
- eBay Groups
- About Me

Buy contains: Registration, Categories, More Ways to Find Items and Buying Resources.

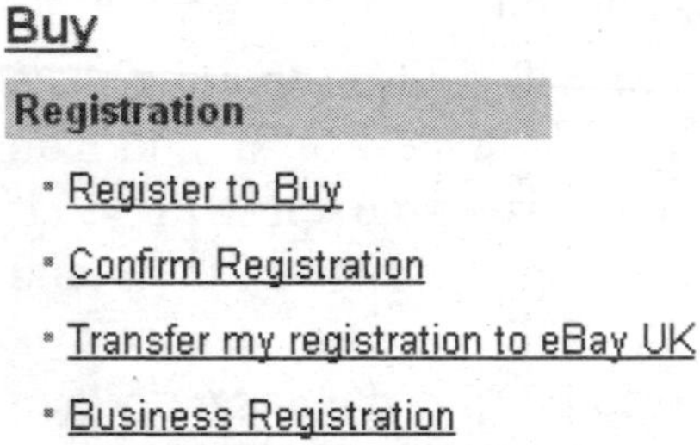

Buy

Registration

- Register to Buy
- Confirm Registration
- Transfer my registration to eBay UK
- Business Registration

Registration gives the link to register as a buyer, the first thing you will do. However, Buy includes innovations enabling buyers to access some fascinating information.

More Ways to Find Items is an example of eBay's pro-active help for buyers. eBay Pulse has been tailored to assist sellers and contains information on popular searches. Completed listings is very useful as it shows auction results and prices achieved.

More Ways to Find Items

- Artist Pages - Movies
- Artist Pages - Music
- Bestselling Artists
- eBay Pulse
- Shops

Sell contains links under two main headings – Selling Resources and Selling Activities.

Sell

Selling Resources

- Seller Protection
- Promotional Tools
- Turbo Lister
- Selling Manager
- Selling Manager Pro
- File Exchange
- Seller Tool Finder
- Picture Manager
- eBay Shops
- eBay Marketplace Research

This shows some of the links available under the Selling Resources list. Many concern established sellers looking to streamline their activities, i.e. Selling Manager and Selling Manager Pro. Turbo Lister is a useful selling tool that allows auction listings to be prepared offline, limiting the online time.

Selling Activities offers a wide range of useful links, including one known as Manage Bidders. This link enables sellers to ensure that they only receive bids from buyers they wish to trade with. It's possible to exclude specific user IDs or categories of buyers, for example those with a feedback score of less than 10 or those who have withdrawn more than 3 bids. It is very flexible!

Selling Activities

- Revise Your Item
- Add to Your Item Description
- Promote Your Item
- Change Your Item's Gallery Image
- Manage Bidders
- Cancel Bids on Your Listing
- End Your Listing
- Relist Your Item
- Manage Your Shop
- View the Status of Your Cross-Promotions
- Manage Your Counters
- Search Want It Now
- Sell Your Past Purchases

The community section of Site Map offers some very useful links, and particularly for feedback. As a new trader you need to tune into the importance of feedback, both yours and other traders.

There has been a big effort to promote the charity side of eBay and Community offers a link to explore this.

Community

Feedback

- Feedback Forum
- View a Member's Feedback
- Leave Feedback for a Member
- Leave Feedback for a Transaction
- Follow Up to Feedback You Left for Others
- Reply to Feedback Received
- Make Feedback Public or Private

Help Topics

- New to eBay
- Finding What You Are Looking For
- Buying
- Selling

The final homepage link is Help. This lists a wide range of topics to solve problems and enhance your trading experiences. More recently it contains Reviews and Guides, an interesting new link.

Problem Solving With Site Map

Let's say you put a SylvaC dog into an auction and a few days later you get a bid. However, being a bit of a 'butter fingers', you drop it onto a tile floor where it smashes into smithereens. Putting aside the emotional and practical side of the trauma you should log onto eBay.co.uk and click onto Site Map and seek out Selling Activities. You will come to a link 'Cancel bids on my item'. This will lead you through the process. Then you need to scan this area once more and select 'End my listing early'. You will be led through a series of simple steps to end your auction.

My eBay and other Home Page Links

home | pay | register | site map

Buy	Sell	My eBay	Community	Help

These links are situated along the top of the home page, just underneath the previous links discussed. They consist of Buy, Sell, My eBay, Community and Help.

Buy – You can initiate a keyword search or opt for an advanced search, a more precise one. You can also browse the categories.

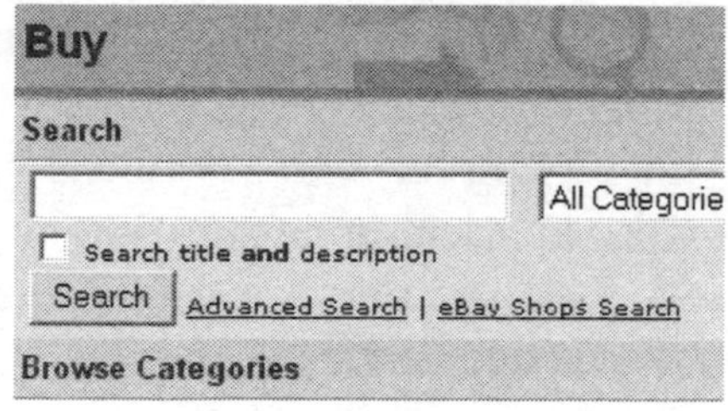

Sell – When you come to create your auction this is where you will start the process.

My eBay – This is another of the most useful areas on the site, your first port of call when logging onto eBay. It is where your browsing, bidding, buying and selling activities are to be found in one convenient spot. No-one else has access to your my eBay. It is so important that it is covered in more detail in Chapter 17.

Community – The strong community spirit on the site is a heartwarming feature. From the early days of trading Pierre Omidyar set up a bulletin board for eBayers to seek and offer advice. This has been extended considerably and there is much to be learned from other eBayer's experiences.

Connect

Discussion Boards

Discuss any eBay-related topic.

Aspiring eBay traders can take advantage of the various educational options on offer in Community. eBay Uni is in full swing at various locations around the UK and provides an ideal opportunity to meet up with traders of all levels. This section also gives details of online workshops and discussion boards.

Help – This area has grown over the years and covers a wide range of topics. Firstly, it offers basic advice on buying and selling. It also has a section with account and billing information. You should come to this area to familiarize yourself with the rules and policies and initiate a violation complaint. In the unfortunate event of a trading problem that requires outside help you should come here to find the appropriate link.

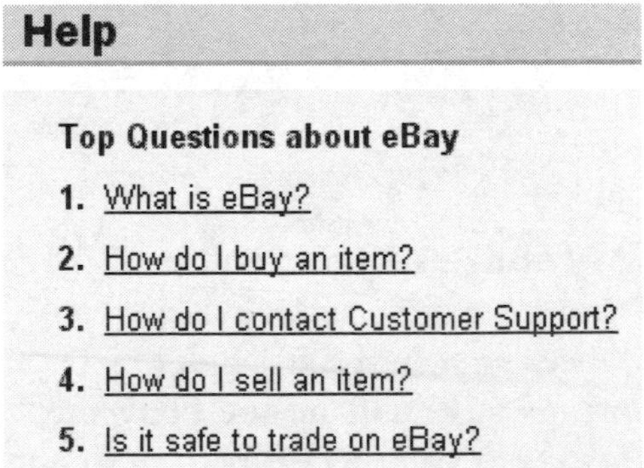

Help

Top Questions about eBay

1. What is eBay?
2. How do I buy an item?
3. How do I contact Customer Support?
4. How do I sell an item?
5. Is it safe to trade on eBay?

4. Feedback

The Idea of Feedback

The jewel in the crown of the eBay site is the feedback forum. It was originally suggested by an eBay customer and has become an indispensable aspect of the online auction process in that it promotes trust and confidence amongst users. The way it operates is that after each transaction both the buyer and seller complete a short sentence about how successful it was. The comments concerning each trader are stored together and available for other buyers and sellers to read. Together the comments build into a profile of the trader and offer clues as to what to expect when dealing with them. It is rather like a high street trader gaining a reputation which can encourage or deter people from using their services, though feedback is much more comprehensive.

How to Find Your Feedback

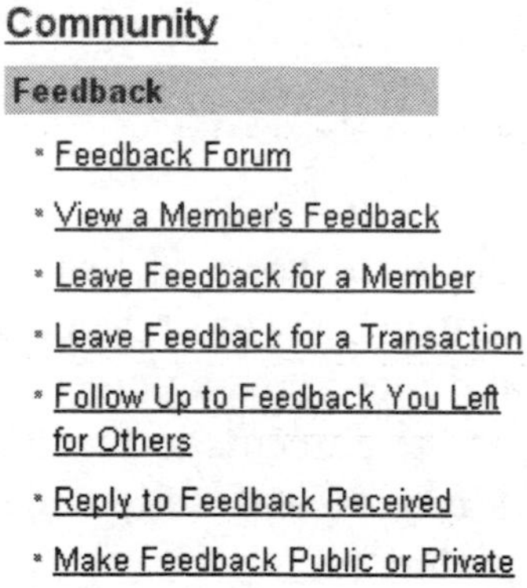

Community

Feedback

- Feedback Forum
- View a Member's Feedback
- Leave Feedback for a Member
- Leave Feedback for a Transaction
- Follow Up to Feedback You Left for Others
- Reply to Feedback Received
- Make Feedback Public or Private

You can reach feedback relating to you and to other members in the Community section of Site Map. These offer links to the various choices. For example you can highlight **Reply to Feedback Received.**

How Feedback Works

Feedback is recorded in two ways:

- Positive, neutral or negative rating
- A free comment on how it went

Rating: ○ Positive ○ Neutral ○ Negative

Comment: [ ]

Positive, neutral or negative feedback. This is expressed as a score and is the difference between the number of members who left a positive rating and the number who left a negative rating. The system only records unique ratings and so if there have been several good transactions, or bad ones, with one trader the feedback is only logged once. The trader below has achieved a score of 44. He has undertaken 50 transactions in total, but those conducted with the same trader do not count towards his score.

Feedback Score:	**44**
Positive Feedback:	**100%**
Members who left a positive:	44
Members who left a negative:	0
All positive feedback received:	50

What is probably of more use to other users is that this score is also expressed as a percentage. Negative feedback is set against positive feedback and represents a percentage of unique ratings. Just glancing at the percentage feedback rating indicates how successful buyers and sellers have been in the eyes of their trading partners.

Feedback Score:	**2431**
Positive Feedback:	**99.9%**
Members who left a positive:	2433
Members who left a negative:	2
All positive feedback received:	3111

The very active trader above has a score of 2431 out of a possible 2433, as two ratings were negative. The feedback percentage is calculated by dividing 2431 by 2433 and multiplying by 100. This gives 99.9%.

Feedback ratings are also presented on a time chart so, if there is any negative feedback, traders can see how recent it is. This trader has received one negative comment in the past six months but two in the past year. They have also received several neutral comments, which do not figure in the percentages but are worth noting.

	Past Month	Past 6 Months	Past 12 Months
positive	169	826	1370
neutral	2	2	3
negative	0	1	1

The aim is, of course, to achieve a 100% positive feedback and it is worth doing everything you can to achieve this. Research on the site has shown that feedback is taken very seriously by buyers and makes a significant difference to the price achieved.

Feedback Free Comment

The second part of feedback consists of a free comment. These are overwhelmingly affirmative and eBay enjoys a convention that a successful outcome to a transaction is rewarded with wild and lavish praise. These exuberant comments represent a fun and idiosyncratic element of eBay. The observations below are very typical:

Fast payment good communications A1

Thanks you fast payment ,highley recommended A++++

great to deal with many thanks

Very FAST payment - great communication - THANKS!! Recommended eBay trader!!!

Lovely person to deal with - highly recommend!

Using Feedback to Your Best Advantage

Before you engage in a transaction with another dealer you should check their feedback to ensure they are reliable. Read the comments carefully and furthermore you should note the timing of the comments. It occasionally happens that an individual trades conscientiously for years but becomes distracted by other matters and slips into bad ways. It does not matter how many successes they have notched up, if the most recent five went wrong you might be best advised to avoid buying from them. The other thing to note about feedback comments is that it can be possible to read between the lines. If a comment reads 'Honest trader, good communicator, highly recommended', it could well mean that something went wrong along the way but the seller ensured that the buyer did not lose out.

Leaving Positive Feedback

In most instances your trading experiences will be good ones and should always be rewarded with praise. You have 90 days following a transaction to leave feedback. It is very easy and there is a link to the comment box in Site Map. However probably the most convenient is situated in My eBay.

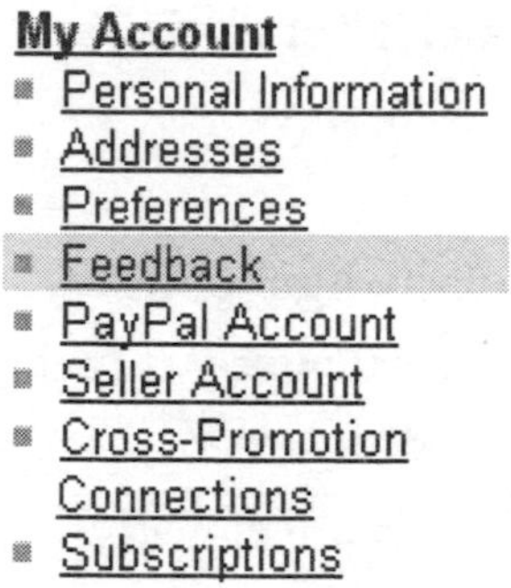

My Account
- Personal Information
- Addresses
- Preferences
- Feedback
- PayPal Account
- Seller Account
- Cross-Promotion Connections
- Subscriptions

You will find this Feedback link on the left-hand side of your **My eBay** and the link below takes you straight into your own feedback forum where you are reminded of transactions awaiting feedback.

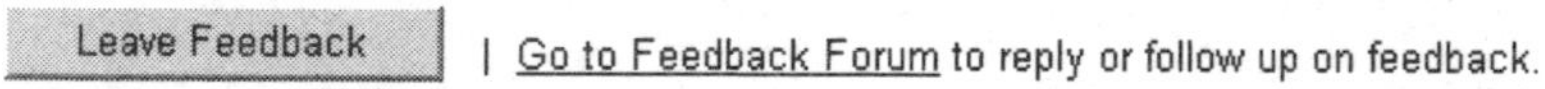

Leave Feedback | Go to Feedback Forum to reply or follow up on feedback.

Leaving Negative Feedback

You should only leave negative feedback as a very last resort and when you are certain of your ground. You cannot edit or retract feedback if you discover you have acted too hastily. You should try everything to resolve matters without resorting to negative feedback as it is permanent and traders hate it. Most traders try to avoid it and if a seller makes a mistake but does everything possible to make amends, they should receive positive feedback – we all make mistakes. However, a very small number of traders are dishonest or chaotic and the feedback system is there to warn other traders about them. The bottom line is that fraudulent traders deserve negative feedback.

How to Ensure Positive Feedback

As A Seller

Remember, your buyer cannot handle the item.
Describe your item very carefully and point out all flaws.
Include as many pictures as necessary, or more!
Ensure you give dimensions.
Draw attention to items that are particularly light or heavy.
Where possible indicate shipping costs, particularly if high.
Send item promptly.
Be attentive to your auctions and answer emails quickly.
Be friendly and honest.

As A Buyer

Check out your seller before you bid.
Read descriptions carefully and do not make assumptions.
Clear up any doubts before you bid by emailing the seller.
If your seller is unhelpful or unfriendly, look elsewhere.
Ensure you can comply with sellers payment requirements.
Send money quickly.
Opt for insurance if it is appropriate.
Check item as soon as it arrives.
Communicate shortcomings immediately and politely.
Step back and consider if you are being fair.

Bear In Mind

Unsubstantiated feedback comments are libelous.

Never get personal, stick to the facts.

There is an opportunity to respond to feedback.

Responding to Negative Feedback

If a trader leaves you negative feedback you can respond. You can leave a statement which sits below their feedback and can often take the sting out of the tail.

Bit Tatty inside

Reply by seller: If you read the description that was stated !!!!!!

Removing Negative Feedback

In most cases feedback is permanent. However is it occasionally possible to have negative feedback removed through Square Trade, the dispute resolution facility. In cases where the negative feedback was left by mistake, and both parties agree, it can be removed. It is also possible for inaccurate and erroneous feedback to be taken away when the other party cannot be contacted. The recipient of this feedback should approach Square Trade and present their grievance. Square Trade will then investigate to discover if there is a case to have the offending phrase removed. You can find the link to Square Trade in Site Map.

4 Feedback

5. PayPal

The Introduction of PayPal

A few years ago the biggest problem for traders wishing to take advantage of eBay's global market was payment. The difficulty and expense of making payments in the required currency often ruled out some transactions and made beginners and occasional buyers wary. Some buyers even resorted to keeping reserves of foreign currencies and sending cash through the post! This has all changed since the development of PayPal, eBay's preferred online payment facility.

Traders have the opportunity to open up a PayPal account for their internet trading. PayPal has made light of former trading obstacles and you can receive funds effortlessly and make payments at the click of a mouse. You need to place a credit card on file and link your PayPal account to a bank account to make the most of this flexible online facility.

It is not surprising that PayPal has rapidly become popular and there are over 100 million account-holding members worldwide in 55 countries. PayPal operates in 6 currencies: Pounds sterling, US Dollars, Canadian Dollars, Australian Dollars, Euros and Japanese Yen. It is ideal for the 'blue moon' user as well as the established trader and the ease it offers undoubtedly attracts buyers. It is particularly helpful for people with limited mobility who cannot easily get to a bank.

PayPal and Security

There are reasons other than security that persuade traders to open a PayPal account. PayPal enables buyers to pay for items without sending cheques, which contain account details, or the necessity to give out credit card numbers.

PayPal itself benefits from encryption technology and offers the greatest possible protection for your private financial details. PayPal offers both Buyer and Seller Protection which makes it a complete and attractive service that all traders should seriously consider.

Advantages of PayPal for Buyers

PayPal is free for buyers.

Sellers are no longer permitted to pass on PayPal charges.

It is quick and convenient.

Cheques, giving account details, are not involved.

The goods are likely to arrive sooner.

It is versatile and can be used for other online transactions.

Qualifying PayPal auctions offer Buyer Protection.

Convenient for people with mobility problems.

Advantages of PayPal for Sellers

Sellers receive money instantly.

With links and reminders it is easy to administer.

Sellers can attract a wide range of foreign buyers.

PayPal offers Seller protection.

The convenience of PayPal draws more buyers.

Qualifying sellers enjoy PayPal Seller Protection.

What Kind of PayPal Account?

Personal Account

- This allows you to send money for free
- Receive money for free on non credit card payments.

Premier Account

- Send money for free
- Receive money for small charge
- Has the benefit of a customer hotline
- Various seller tools.

Business Account

- All of the above plus it offers multiple logins
- Allows you to do business under a corporate name.

Though free, the personal account only offers limited services and traders often decide to upgrade to a premier account. The premier account is suitable for all non-professional traders.

PayPal Fees

It is free to open an account.

Buyers send money free of charge.

Small traders are charged 3.4% of total money plus 20p.

High volume traders are charged from 1.4% plus 20p depending on the seller's successful application.

Fees for Transferring Money from your PayPal Account to your Bank Account

It is free to transfer £50 or more.

It costs 25p to transfer £49.99 or less.

Requirements for a PayPal Account

To set up a PayPal account you require:

- Email address
- Phone number
- Credit card or debit card
- Bank account details.

(Linking your account to a bank account and adding a credit card allows you to make full use of PayPal.)

Overview of Setting Up a PayPal Account

- Select the link to Initiate PayPal Registration
- Complete the form
- Think of a password
- Receive PayPal email
- Enter your password
- Add credit card and bank details.

You can use PayPal with specified financial limitations

- Follow instructions specific to you to verify your account
- Your status changes from 'unverified' to 'verified'.

You can use PayPal with no financial limitation

A PayPal account is free to set up. Buyers are not charged to use PayPal but sellers pay a small fee.

Steps to Opening a PayPal Account

Log on to www.paypal.co.uk

Click on **Sign up for your free PayPal account**

Join PayPal Today
Now Over 100 million accounts

Personal or Business Account

You need to choose between a Personal, Premier and Business Account. The most practical for new traders is the Premier Account which allows buyers to pay with their credit cards.

Personal Account
Ideal for online shoppir
secure network. Persoı
payments. Learn more

Premier Account
Perfect for buying and
payment types for low

Business Account
The right choice for yo
fees. Do business unde

Completing the PayPal Form

The new screen appears and you are required to enter your details into the boxes:

- Name & address
- Telephone number
- Email address
- Think up a password
- Security questions e.g. school attended
- Type of account
- Enter security numbers
- **Review the information and sign up.**

First Name: Ronald
Last Name: Speed
Address 1: The Old Barn
Address 2: (optional) King
Town/City:
County: Somerset
Postal code:
Country: United Kingdom
y of Residence: United Kingdom
me Telephone: (Why is thi
ork Telephone: (optional)

ess and Password - Your email address will be u
at least **eight characters long** and is case sensi
urage you to use a brand new password and NOT o

Email Address:

Receive an email from PayPal

This confirms your email address and offers a link to continue the process.

service@paypal.c...Activate Your PayPal Account.

Open the email and click on the link to proceed.

Enter your password as directed and confirm.

Viewing Your PayPal Account

This reveals your new, unverified, PayPal account.

Status: UK - Unverified (New)

Balance Manage | Transfer	
Pound Sterling (Primary):	£0.00 GBP
US Dollars:	$0.00 USD
Current Total in Pounds Sterling:	£0.00 GBP

View Limits

By clicking on to the **View Limits** link you can discover your pre-verification sending limit.

Your Sending Limit is:

This limit varies from £0 to over £1,000 and requires you to add your credit card and bank account details to activate.

Add a credit card by clicking onto **Add Credit Card** found in the **Activate Account** box on the left-hand side of your Account Overview.

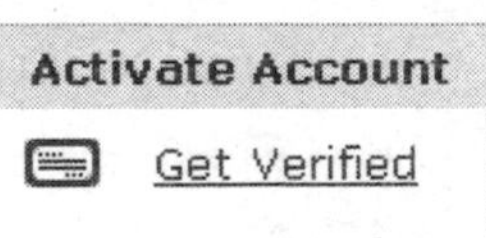

Completing the Registration Process

It is important to verify your account. The verification process varies from person to person and you need to follow the instructions.

Using PayPal before being Verified

You do not have to wait until you are verified to start using PayPal, you can take advantage straight away. However, financial restrictions will apply and this limit is specific to you. You will be informed about your limit when you register, as discussed. As soon as you have completed the application process and your status has been verified you can enjoy full use of the PayPal service, providing that you maintain a current debit or credit card on file.

Steps to Verify Your PayPal Account

Set up Bank funding

Validate your account information

Supply merchant information.

Robin Plate - one of a set of six of World Wildlife Fund plates by Ursula Band. This sold for £9.50 in an eBay auction. It was paid for using PayPal within minutes of the end of the auction and was received by the buyer the very next day!

How to Reach Your PayPal Account

To take a look at your account enter www.paypal.co.uk into your browser – this brings up the home page, as shown below. (Take a minute to look over the various options as it gives an idea of the versatility of PayPal.)

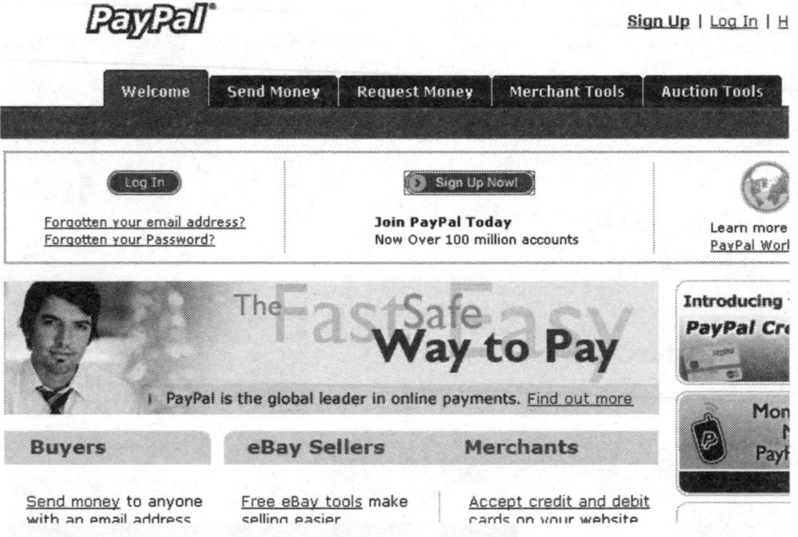

Enter your email address and password into the Member Log In. Your email address may already be there – if so you just need to enter your password.

Click on Log In.

Member Login

Registered users log in here. Be sure

Email Address: cherryberry@ac

Password:

Inside Your PayPal Account

You are now inside your own PayPal account. This is private to you and protected by your password. It is very important that you do not share your password with anyone and that you change it frequently to keep your account safe. PayPal staff will never ask you for your password and any such request must be viewed as suspicious.

The account below is a Premier Account and probably the most usual for part-time traders. From this page you can initiate all activities to do with your PayPal account. It is very quick, easy and convenient.

Log Out | Hel

My Account | Send Money | Request Money | Merchant Tools | Auction Tools

Overview | Add Funds | Withdraw | History | Resolution Centre | Profile

This opening page of your account gives your account balance. The account below holds £229.67 and $3.90 (US dollars). This is expressed as a total in pounds £231.74. Some traders like to hold money in different currencies, though this account holder could just as easily change it all into pounds.

Balance Manage | Transfer	
Pound Sterling (Primary):	£229.67 GBP
US Dollars:	$3.90 USD
Current Total in Pounds Sterling:	£231.74 GBP

Checking Transaction Details and Charges

This opening account page also contains details of payments you have made and received through PayPal. You can select the information you wish to view. Payments are clearly set out giving the type of transfer, the name of the other party, and the date, etc. You can also choose to view just your buying or selling activities.

Recent Activity | All Activity | Items Won ebY

Your Recent Activity displays the past days of account activity.

File	Type	To/From	Name/Email/Phone	Date	Status
☐	Payment	To	lisa fisher	26 Apr. 2006	Completed

Each transaction is clearly listed for ease of understanding. The top row of the list below shows costs relating to a buying transaction. The first figure shows £7.40, the sum transferred to the seller. The second column shows PayPal charges and in this case is a nil figure because it was a buying transaction and the buyer is not charged. The third column shows the net sum, which is therefore unchanged. The final column shows the account balance, which has been reduced by £7.40, the sum that was transferred.

In the next row the gross sum transferred is £17.70. However, as this sum was transferred into the account resulting from a selling transaction, the seller is charged £0.89. This means the net sum of £16.81 is transferred into the sellers account. The final column reflects this increase.

Details		-£7.40 GBP	£0.00 GBP	-£7.40 GBP	£284.71 GBP
Details		£17.70 GBP	-£0.89 GBP	£16.81 GBP	£292.11 GBP

Transferring Funds to Your Bank

You need to Log On to your account using your password.

Check the balance and decide how much you want to transfer. In this example we will transfer £29.67.

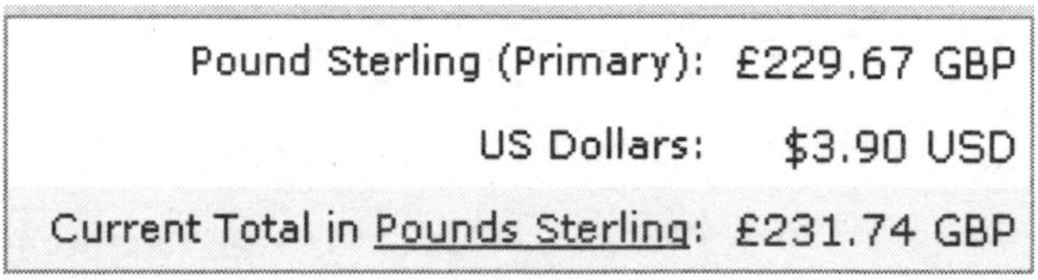

Pound Sterling (Primary):	£229.67 GBP
US Dollars:	$3.90 USD
Current Total in Pounds Sterling:	£231.74 GBP

Take the cursor to the top of the page to the row of links shown below and select **Withdraw**.

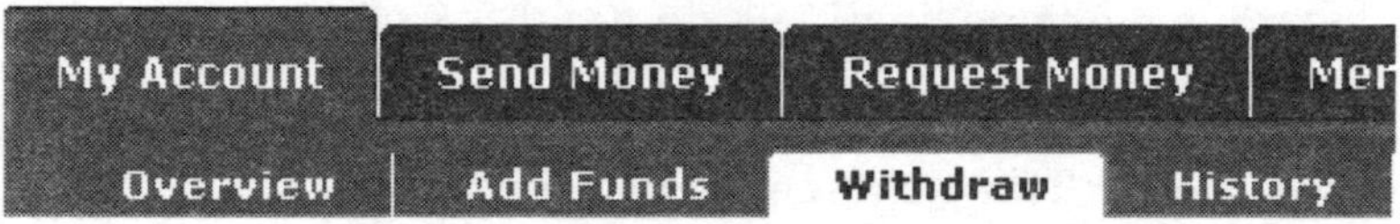

My Account | Send Money | Request Money | Mer

Overview | Add Funds | Withdraw | History

This brings up the page as shown below.

You should select **Transfer funds to your bank account.**

(Please note that it takes several working days for the money to appear in your account.)

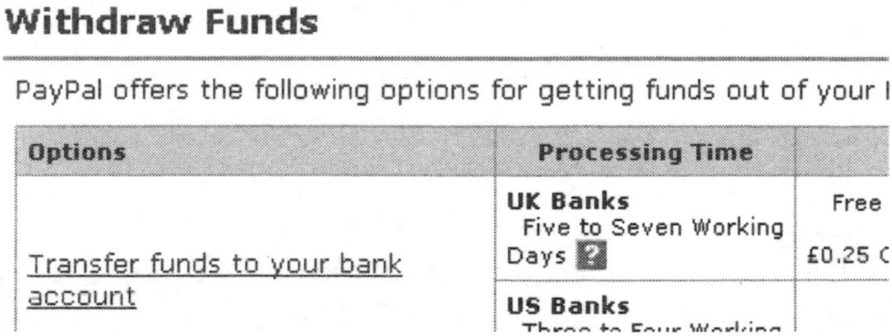

Withdraw Funds

PayPal offers the following options for getting funds out of your I

Options	Processing Time	
Transfer funds to your bank account	**UK Banks** Five to Seven Working Days	Free £0.25 C
	US Banks Three to Four Working	

Account Balance. A new page appears that gives your balance as shown below. You are given the opportunity to check the account number (it only gives the last four figures of your bank account number as a security precaution).

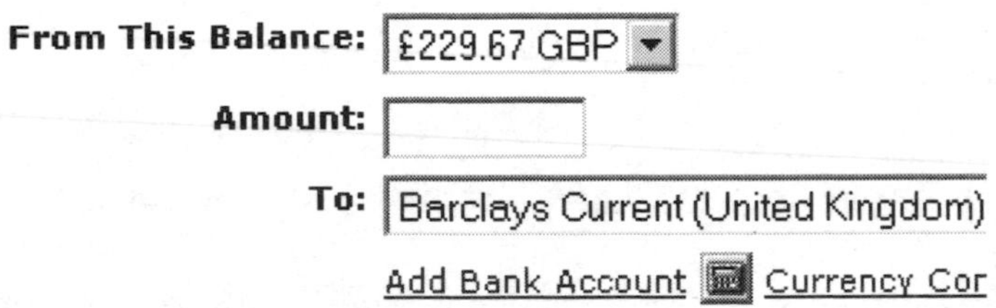

Type in the amount your wish to transfer, as shown below. (Only give numbers involved, do not use £ sign)

Because this transaction involves a sum of less than £50 there will be a charge of £0.25. This charge is shown clearly in the financial details before the transfer, as below.

Check the details and select continue.

Amount:	£29.67 GBP
Withdrawal Fee:	-£0.25 GBP
Amount to Bank Account:	£29.42 GBP

Regular sellers can easily avoid the withdrawal fee by waiting until they have accumulated £50.

Your new balance will immediately reflect the transfer of funds out of your PayPal Account. You can go back to the PayPal home page to check this.

Balance Manage | Transfer	
Pound Sterling (Primary):	£200.00 GBP
US Dollars:	$3.90 USD
Current Total in Pounds Sterling:	£202.07 GBP

The details of this transferal of funds will be confirmed to you in an email. It will arrive with your incoming email very soon after the transaction is complete.

service@paypal.c...PayPal Electronic Funds Transfer

Identifying Sellers Who Accept PayPal

You can spot the auction listings that welcome PayPal payment because they display the PayPal symbol, as below.

BRAVEMOUTH, Living with Billy Connolly by P. Stephenson

However, not only do the traders below accept payment through PayPal, their buyers are covered for PayPal Buyer Protection. This is indicated by the shield next to the PayPal sign. This is the service offered to eligible PayPal traders, discussed later.

My Auto-Biography by Charlie Chaplin

MARY Queen of Scots, 1971, Antonia Fraser

How to Pay Using PayPal

Five simple steps to paying for an item with PayPal.

1. Open eBay Item Won! Email or sellers invoice
2. Review Purchase
3. Note Payment Details
4. Confirm Your Payment
5. Receive email from PayPal confirming payment.

1. Open eBay Item Won! email or seller's invoice

Auction winners receive an email from eBay. There are different ways to start the payment process, from eBay winners email, sellers invoice or go to My eBay.

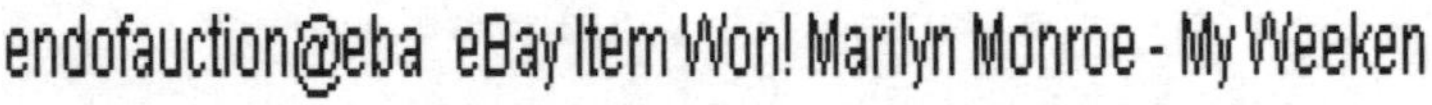

endofauction@eba eBay Item Won! Marilyn Monroe - My Weeken

Open the email, which begins by congratulating you on winning this item. It gives information about the sale and includes payment instructions. Click on **Pay Now.**

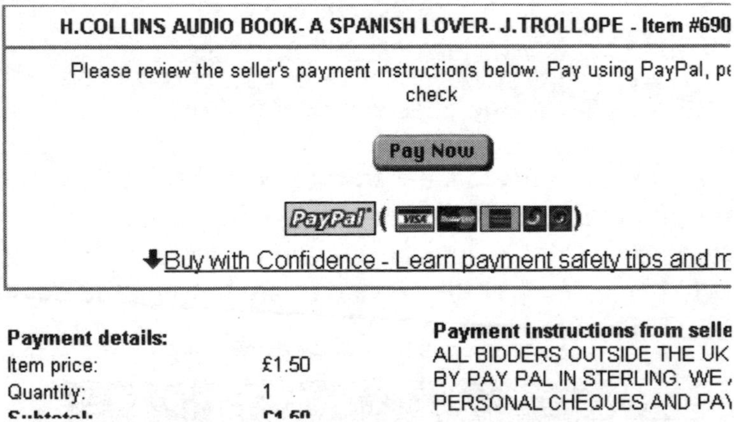

H.COLLINS AUDIO BOOK- A SPANISH LOVER- J.TROLLOPE - Item #690

Please review the seller's payment instructions below. Pay using PayPal, pe check

Pay Now

PayPal ( )

Buy with Confidence - Learn payment safety tips and m

Payment details:

Item price:	£1.50
Quantity:	1

Payment instructions from selle
ALL BIDDERS OUTSIDE THE UK BY PAY PAL IN STERLING. WE , PERSONAL CHEQUES AND PA\

2. Review Your Purchase

This takes you to Review Your Purchase where you will find details of both price and Postage and Packing costs. When you state shipping costs in your auction they are automatically reflected in your invoices. You need to check that the correct amounts have been included. If you have offered your buyer a shipping discount for multiple purchases you need to ensure they are correct. If you need to make an adjustment you can type it in and select recalculate and the new total will automatically appear.

	Qty.	Price	Subtotal
VER- J.TROLLOPE	1	£1.50	£1.50
Postage and packing via Royal Mail 1st Class Standard:			£1.50
Postal insurance: (not offered)			--
Seller discounts (-) or charges (+):			-0.00
Total:			£3.00
			recalculate

If the amounts include postage and packing, and are correct, you should go to the bottom of the page and click on the link **Continue** or select the **Pay Now** PayPal link as shown below.

Thank you for purchasing my item.

I accept the following payment methods:

3. Payment Details

You have now reached the secure payment processor for your seller. The padlock symbol, shown here, will appear in the top right-hand side of the page and denotes a secure page.

Secure Transaction

Once again you should check that the amounts are listed correctly.

	Qty	Price	Subtotal
UDIO BOOK- A /ER- J.TROLLOPE	1	£1.50 GBP	£1.50 GBP

UK Postage & Packing via Royal Mail 1st Class Standard to TA9XX (includes any seller packing fees) : 1.50

UK Insurance (optional): 0.00

VAT : 0.00

Towards the bottom of the page is the PayPal Log in section. You need to check that your email address is correct and then enter your password. This security check ensures that only you can make a payment from your PayPal account.

PayPal Log in

Email Address: cherry999@aol.com Problems logging in?

PayPal Password: ●●●●●●●● Forget your password?

Locate and select the **Continue** button at the bottom right-hand side of this page.

Confirm Your Payment

This page gives financial details of the purchase.

Item Title	Qty	Price	Subtotal
H.COLLINS AUDIO BOOK- A SPANISH LOVER- J.TROLLOPE	1	£1.50 GBP	£1.50 GBP

UK Postage & Packing via Royal Mail 1st Class Standard to TA9XX (includes any seller packing fees) :	£1.50 GBP
UK Insurance (optional):	£0.00 GBP
Total:	£3.00 GBP

Source of Funds

Whilst there are funds in your PayPal account payment will be taken from there. Any shortfall will be charged to your credit card. The source of funds is shown as above.

Source of Funds

Pound Sterling Balance: £3.00 GBP

Postage Information

(•) **Send to** The Old Barn,, Kingsw
Add Address

( ) **No delivery address required**

You should check the postal address.

There is also an opportunity to send a message to the seller.

Message to Seller (Optional)

```
Looking forward to receiving the book.  Thanks so
much.
Cherry
```

To continue, press Pay at the bottom of the page.

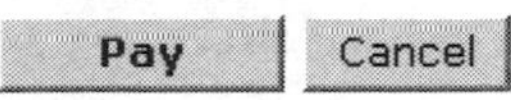

PayPal Payment Complete

This concludes the transaction with a final page confirming that you have made a secure payment.

You Made A Payment

Payment Information

You have sent a secure payment of for the eBay it
receipt for this transaction shortly.

Shortly afterwards a receipt will arrive from PayPal in the form of an email. You should store this safely away as evidence of payment. In the unlikely event of a dispute you will need all relevant paperwork to support your claim.

11/07/2004 service@paypal.c...Receipt for Your Payment to stell

Changing Details of Your PayPal Account

There may be times when you need to make changes to your account (for instance, a new email address) or take advantage of wider PayPal features. Such activities are easily undertaken and you should start by selecting Profile (bottom right) from the row of options at the top of your account page. This reveals the list of options shown below.

Request Money | Merchant Tools | Auction Tools

Withdraw | History | Resolution Centre | **Profile**

They are convenient links to making the desired changes. They are grouped in three sections, according to the type of alteration you wish to make, Account Information, Financial Information and Selling Preferences.

The options given under the Account section include the link to changing your password. You will need to do this frequently as a means of keeping your account safe.

It also contains a Notifications link to enable you to control which you receive as below.

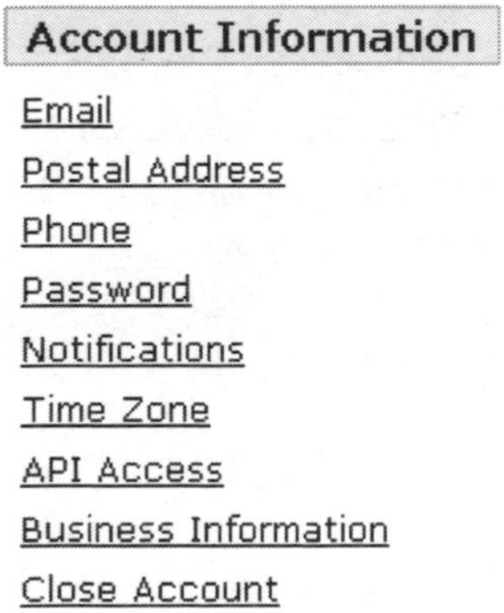

Account Information

Email
Postal Address
Phone
Password
Notifications
Time Zone
API Access
Business Information
Close Account

Payment Notifications

Please send me an email when:

- [x] I receive money with PayPal
- [x] I request money with PayPal
- [x] I receive PayPal Website Paym

You can opt to receive all or none as well as other PayPal notifications.

Profile is also the area to visit when you want to make changes to your financial set-up. You can change and update credit cards and alter the bank account that connects to your PayPal account.

Financial Information

Credit Cards

Bank Accounts

Currency Balances

Redeem Gift Certificates and Points

Monthly Account Statements

Merchant-Initiated Payments

Selling Preferences

Auctions

Value Added Tax

Postage Calculations

Payment Receiving Preferences

Instant Payment Notification Preferences

Reputation

Seller Eligibility for PayPal Buyer Protection

Website Payment Preferences

Encrypted Payment Settings

Custom Payment Pages

Invoice Templates

Language Encoding

Profile is also the start point for making changes to your selling preferences and the way in which your high bidders are automatically contacted after an auction. This is where you will come to check on your eligibility to offer your buyers PayPal Buyer Protection. These links are quick and convenient and allow you to tailor the auction process.

6. Getting Organised

The Strategy for Success

eBay offers a wonderful opportunity to trade globally and you need to prepare and consider your approach. It is best to start gently and build up experiences gradually. I would suggest the following strategy for beginners:

- For your first ten transactions simply focus on your feedback. You need to secure 10 positive feedback comments to earn the trust of other traders. Bear in mind that if one of your initial transactions results in negative feedback it will look bad when expressed as a percentage and put other eBayers off trading with you.

- Do not sell anything of any real value until you have 10 positive feedback comments because you will probably not achieve the best possible price. Make your initial sales modest items that are easy to describe accurately.

- It is best to start with a buying transaction – it is easier than selling and will break you in gently. It is important for a seller to understand how it feels on the other side of the counter.

- I recommend that your first transactions are undertaken within this country as there is so much that is familiar to you – don't forget your main concern is feedback.

- If the transaction goes well but your trading partner forgets to post positive feedback in response to yours, you should email them and politely ask for it explaining that you are trying to build up your feedback rating. eBayers are very kind and this will probably do the trick.

- Make your initial transactions simple ones, nothing fragile, badly damaged or bulky. These things add a small amount of risk to a transaction and are best tackled when you have gained confidence.

- The vast majority of trading communication is conducted by email. Though this mostly works well it can be difficult to gauge the tone of a message. It is advisable to exaggerate courtesy in order to avoid any misunderstanding.

- Make your auction sound as friendly as possible and encourage buyers to email you with queries. People buy from people they like and so any chance to make contact can be turned to your advantage.

Who Can Register?

Anyone can browse on eBay but in order to buy and sell you need to be at least 18 and you have to register. It is quick and easy and free. There are two kinds of registration, as a buyer and as a seller.

You need to have the following to hand:

- Name
- Address & Post Code
- Telephone number
- Email address
- User name
- Password.

To Register as a Seller

You need all above plus:

- A debit or credit card
- Bank account details.

Why Give Your Card Details?

eBay need a credit card to identify sellers and ensure they are over 18.

Sellers can choose the Payment Method from:

Direct Debit. This is a convenient method but only open to users with UK bank accounts. It requires a signed authorization mandate and offers unlimited access to sell.

Credit Card on File – Allows unlimited access to sell.

Pay-as-you-go. You can pay your monthly invoice by cheque or one-off credit card payment. However without a credit card on file for automatic monthly billing you will be limited to £15 before your listing activity is blocked.

How to Register to Buy & Sell

Registering to Buy

Click link to Register on the home page.

Registration: Enter Information

1 Enter Information   2 Agree to Terms   3 Confirm Your Email

First name: Ronald   Last name: Speed

Street address: 12 Badger Place

Complete form with the following details:

Name, address & post code

Telephone number & Email address

User ID

Password

Secret question & Date of Birth.

Read & Agree to Terms

Receive an email from eBay

eBay just sent you an email to **percy@riversi**

Click on the link, shown below (or if it does not work copy it into the browser)

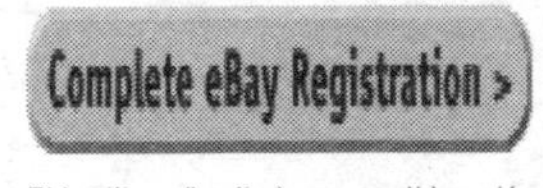

Registering to Sell

Click on **Sell** link.

Enter your User ID & Password

1. Verify Information

Name, Address & Telephone number

Date of Birth.

2. Enter Credit or Debit Card Details

It is an exercise in identification and so the address must match that on your monthly statements.

3. Enter Bank Details

Bank name

Sort Code

Bank account number.

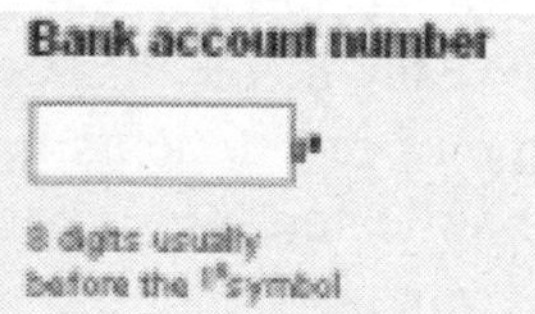

(This is for identification rather then payment purposes. Funds are not deducted from your account without your authorization.)

4. Select How to Pay Seller Fees

Note - You can change the payment method at any time to suit you.

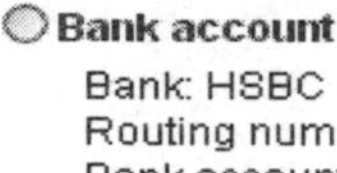

Registration Complete – you can now sell on eBay.

Choosing a Password

Choose a password carefully as it should not be anything obvious. You might want to use a mix of letters and numbers. Do not share your password with anyone else and change it at regular intervals. eBay staff will never ask you for your password and so if you receive an email asking for it, you should be cautious as it is a fraudulent attempt to get access to your details. You should forward the email to www.spoof.com where they will investigate it.

Selecting a User Name

When selecting a user name, the nickname by which you are known to other traders, give it some thought. It needs to be something that you can live with happily. It should also be fairly easy to recall as you will be using it a great deal and some of my students have made the mistake of making it so complicated that it becomes a burden. It is possible to change your user name but it is not recommended as it is part of your identity.

Example of a user name: mollygilly882

Organising Finances

It is a good idea to give some thought to the money side of things at the very beginning. Even non-professional traders prefer to open up a new bank account for their eBay finances and link all incomings and outgoings to it. You can arrange a debit card for this account and use it to pay eBay's fees. It means that your eBay trading activities are separate and easy to monitor. It might surprise you see how easily you can build up a small nest egg for that charity donation, car, holiday or leg wax.

Please note – all businesses are liable for tax and if your activities qualify you may require specialist advice.

Create an eBay Picture Folder

It is a good idea to open up an **eBay Selling** folder for your eBay pictures to keep them all in one place. I would recommend that you also open up an **eBay Sold** folder. This means that you can easily transfer pictures into this folder when the item has sold and change the file name to incorporate the price it achieved. Over the years this will build up into a useful completed auction portfolio that you will find fascinating.

How to create an eBay Selling folder:

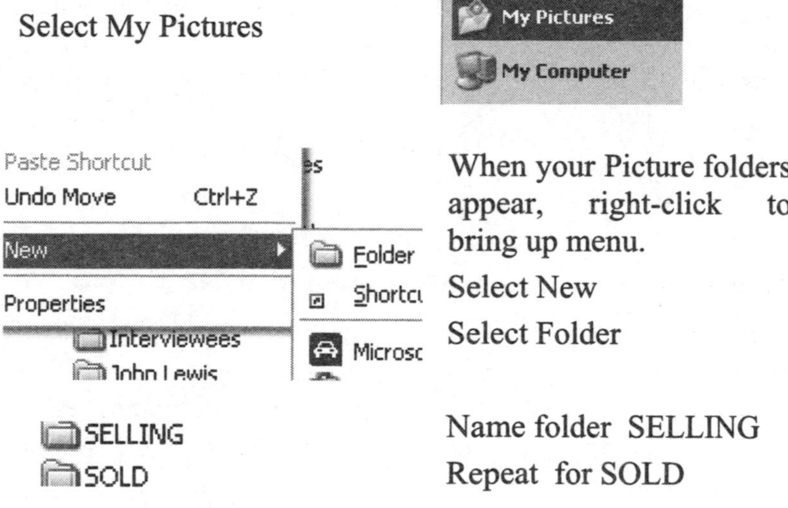

Click on Start

Select My Pictures

When your Picture folders appear, right-click to bring up menu.

Select New

Select Folder

Name folder SELLING

Repeat for SOLD

If your selling activities are extensive you can create a Sold file each year.

Transferring Pictures to your Sold File

You should create your Sold file as you go whilst the final prices are fresh in your mind. You can add this task to your selling routine and mentally link it to leaving feedback.

Locate the picture in the Selling file and highlight by resting the cursor on it.

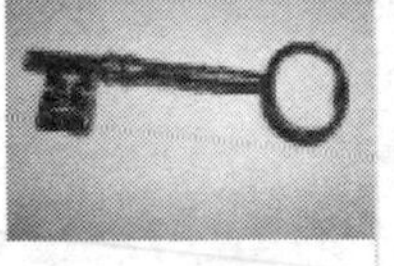

Old Key

Move cursor to the left side of screen

Select **Move this File** option

When the file browser appears select the Sold file.

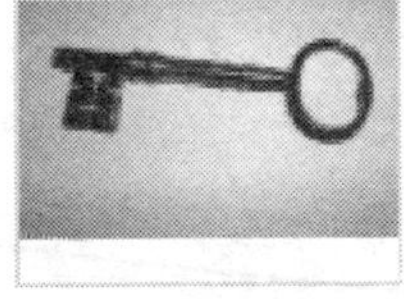

£6 June 06

Take the cursor to Rename this file on left-hand side of screen and select.

Rename the image with the price achieved and date.

7. Finding Things

Finding What You Want

There are literally millions of items for sale in eBay auctions at any one time and it is highly likely that there is something that is perfect for you - the trick is to find it. You have two options for searching:

Browsing the Categories

If you do not know exactly what you are looking for you can casually cruise the categories. For example, let's suppose you decide to give up your job and become a rock star. You will need a guitar and frankly there is no better place to find one than on eBay.

Categories
Antiques & Art
Automotive
Books, Comics & Magazines
Business, Office & Industrial
Clothes, Shoes & Accessories
Coins
Collectables
Computing
Consumer Electronics
Dolls & Bears
DVDs, Film & TV
Home, Garden & Family
Jewellery & Watches
Mobile & Home Phones
Music
Musical Instruments NEW!
PC & Video Gaming
Photography

Firstly locate the categories list on the left-hand side of the home page. Scan down until you come across the **Musical Instruments** category – position the cursor over this and click. This takes you into the musical instruments category which consists of lots of different sub-categories.

Sub-categories

You will find a section for every different kind of instrument. There is a specific section for each type of guitar – find **Bass.**

Musical Instruments

Search within **Musical Inst**

Search in United Kingdom

Brass
Cornet
French Horn
Trombone
Trumpet
Tuba/ Baritone/
Euphonium
Other Brass
Guitars
Accessories
Acoustic
Bass
Electric
Electro-Acoustic

Percussion
Accessories
Cymbals
Drums
Tambourines
Other Percussion
Pro Audio/ Equipment
Amplifiers
Cables/ Leads
Computer Recording
Drum Machines
Microphones
Mixers/ Mixer

Position your cursor over **Bass** and click. It will reveal the current auctions of bass guitars as shown below.

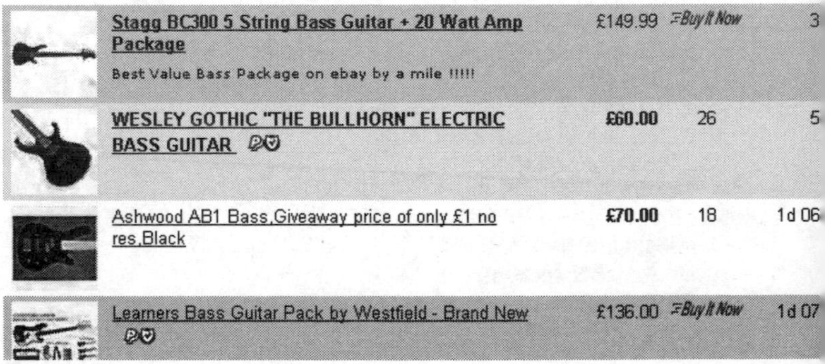

Stagg BC300 5 String Bass Guitar + 20 Watt Amp Package — £149.99 Buy It Now
Best Value Bass Package on ebay by a mile !!!!!

WESLEY GOTHIC "THE BULLHORN" ELECTRIC BASS GUITAR — £60.00 — 26

Ashwood AB1 Bass,Giveaway price of only £1 no res,Black — £70.00 — 18 — 1d 06

Learners Bass Guitar Pack by Westfield - Brand New — £136.00 Buy It Now — 1d 07

Looking at an Auction

If there is an auction that looks interesting you can position your cursor over the title, click the mouse, and it will take you into the auction itself, as shown below.

WESLEY GOTHIC "THE BULLHORN" ELECTRIC BASS

You are signed in

Go to larger picture

Current bid:	**£60.00**
	Place Bid >
Time left:	**4 hours 1 mins** 5-day listing Ends 13-Jun-04 20:05:06 BST
Start time:	08-Jun-04 20:05:06 BST
History:	26 bids (£1.00 starting bid)

Each auction usually contains one or more pictures of the item as well as a description, example below. You should take time to study it carefully giving particular attention to information about condition.

Wesley 'The Bullhorn' Electric Bass Guitar

Brand new Wesley Bullhorn Electric Bass Guitar (Model MBG-332)
instrument with a chunky deep down bass sound and snug feelin

All our instruments come fully setup and inspected to ensure the

Features:

- Hard Wood Body & Hard Maple Neck
- 24 fret rosewood fingerboard
- Full Scale 864mm
- Twin Soapbar Pickups

Key Word Search

One of the advantages of buying on eBay is that you do not have to spend time browsing - you can target your search. This can be done by using eBay's own search engine and your choice of key words.

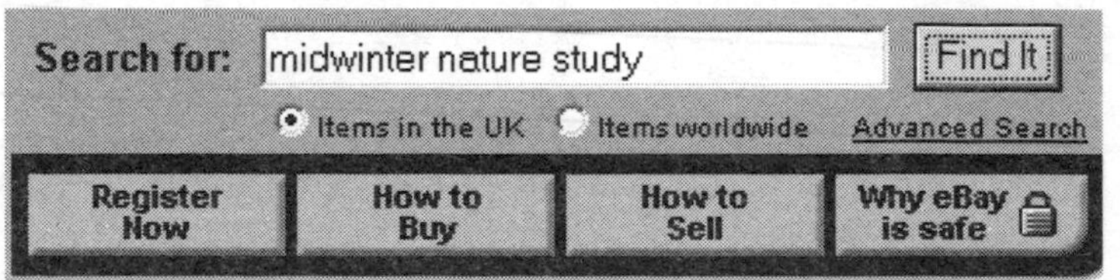

For example, let's say you are a keen collector of a particular pattern of Midwinter tablewares called Nature Study. You do not want to browse the Midwinter category because Nature Study is the only design that you collect. You can set up a targeted search by going to eBay's home page. Towards the top you will find the Search for facility. You should type in **midwinter nature study**, as shown above. Upper and lower case make no difference on eBay.

Items in the UK or Items Worldwide

You need to decide if you want to search for items worldwide or just within the UK. In the example above the UK has been selected but you can click in the Items worldwide circle.

Advanced Search - If you click on Advanced Search it will bring up a page that allows you to enter some very specific requirements including price parameters.

Continuing with the Key Word Search

However, if you continue with the midwinter nature study search it will reveal the current auctions of Midwinter Nature Study, as shown above. In fact it will reveal all the auctions that contain these words in their title. As before, with the browsing method, you can enter a particular auction by positioning the cursor on the title and clicking the mouse.

Item	Price
MIDWINTER NATURE STUDY TEA SET	£51.00
MIDWINTER NATURE STUDY SMALL BOWL TERENCE CONRAN N/R	£7.00
MIDWINTER NATURE STUDY LARGE BOWL TERENCE CONRAN N/R	£4.99
MIDWINTER NATURE STUDY LARGE PLATE TERENCE CONRAN	£28.00

If the search is not satisfactory you can return to the home page and adapt your search by using different words. You need to think laterally and try different options. Also you have to bear in mind that different countries use different expressions.

Extend the Key Word Search to Title and Description

A standard key word search links up with the title. It is possible to extend this to search title and description. In the example below putting Nicole Kidman in the search box reveals 486 current auctions. By ticking Search title **and** description this increases to 1441 items.

All Items | Auctions | Buy It Now

Nicole Kidman | DVD, Film & TV

☑ Search title **and** description

DVDs Finder
Region
Any

1441 items found for **Nicole Kidman** in
Located in: United Kingdom Show all

Try Different Spellings

Another tip is to experiment with a variety of spellings and mis-spellings. Key word searches simply bring up the words as they are entered and there are frequently instances of incorrect spelling.

A key word search **Toni Raymond** revealed 68 auctions.

TONI RAYMOND BUTTER DISH

However a key word search **Tony Raymond** came up with just 3. It is likely that these auctions will be viewed by a restricted number of buyers and it is your opportunity to snap up a bargain.

Tony Raymond Tea Canister

Refining Your Search

One of the best aspects of buying on eBay is that you can tailor your search. You can use the list of options on the left-hand side to ensure that the auctions revealed fit into your criteria. For example you can choose to see only:

Items Listed with PayPal – increasing numbers of buyers are opting to use PayPal and some only consider items with this payment option.

Buy It Now Items – some buyers only view items that they can buy instantly.

Items near to me – if you are looking for a grand piano or pool table you might prefer to buy within your region.

Completed listings – reveals auctions that have ended. You cannot bid on these items but it shows the price that was achieved and is very useful information for buyers and sellers. Many sellers research the completed prices to help them determine start price and decide what selling enhancements to include in their auction.

Listings Starting today – you can view new listings or cut the wait and bring up auctions that are coming to a close.

Items priced – you can view auctions for items that exactly fit your price band.

Customise Your Search

There is much you can do to pinpoint your search. You can alter the options to suit your exact requirements. These are revealed by clicking onto **Customise options displayed above**, below **Show Items.**

Buy It Now items
Items near me
Bristol (Change)
Completed listings
Items priced
to
Show Items
Customise options displayed above.

This brings up the page as shown below. You can include or exclude your selections by highlighting them and the appropriate arrows.

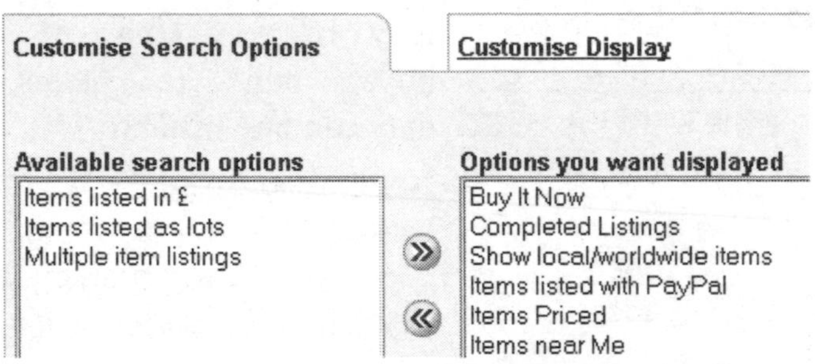

Searches can be worldwide or restricted to your locality. They can be simple and general or meticulously honed. I have bought specific but inexpensive items for my antiques and collectables classes from places as far away as New Zealand and the USA. Before eBay such a comprehensive armchair search was not possible.

8. Bidding & Paying

Important - Before You Place a Bid

When you have discovered something exciting in an auction your first thought might be to place a bid. You should resist the urge to act hastily as there are three things that you need to do to ensure that things go well.

- Investigate the seller
- Discover the required payment methods
- Check on cost of shipping

1. Investigate the seller. You will find the seller's details on the right-hand side of their auction page. This will give the all-important feedback rating that was discussed in Chapter 4. This seller has interacted with 45 other traders and all have awarded positive feedback This seller appears to be someone you can trust.

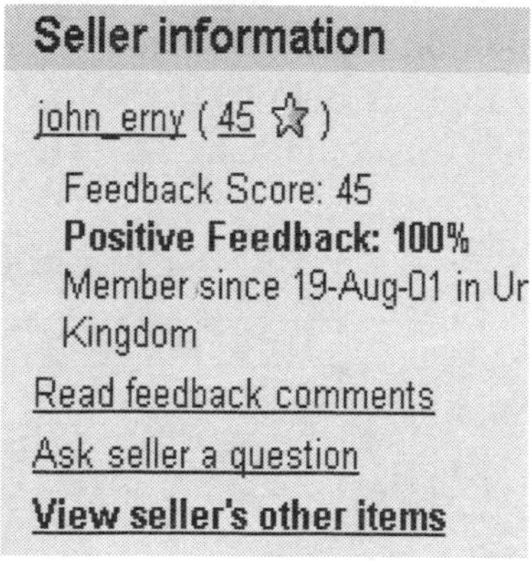

Occasionally good traders receive negative feedback and you need to weigh it all up and consider the bigger picture. You can make use of the **Read feedback comments** option, as shown above, to read the comment and the response, and decide for yourself.

2. You need to discover the methods by which they accept payment. Some traders only accept one form of payment and you need to ensure you can meet their requirements. The trader, below, offers a range of options.

Payment methods accepted

- PayPal*
- Personal cheque
- Postal Order or Banker's Draft
- Credit card

3. It is wise to check on the cost of postage and packing as this varies considerably. Some traders charge actual postage, with no packaging or handling charges, whilst full-time eBayer traders buy their packaging materials and have to pass this additional cost on. It is best to read the auction details to check if the postage and packing costs are stated, as below. If they are not mentioned in the auction you can contact the seller to discover what they will be.

HANDLING CHARGES ON THIS ITEM

DESTINATION	HANDLING CHARGE
United Kingdom	5 GB POUNDS
European Union (EEC)	10 GB POUNDS
Rest of the World (inc USA)	10 GB POUNDS

Ask Seller a Question

You should take the opportunity of clearing up any doubts about the item or terms of sale before you place a bid. Bids are legally binding and if you end up as the high bidder you are obliged to go through with the purchase.

Ask seller a question

How to Place a Bid

Bidding on eBay auction is easy and convenient, millions of people do it every week. You can bid in two ways:

- By increment
- By proxy.

Bidding by Increment

For example, let's suppose that you want to buy these irresistible Midwinter dishes.

Place Bid >

To place a bid you need to click on the link on the auction page. This brings up the bidding form, below.

You should place your bid in the space provided and click continue. Type in the numbers only, no £ sign.

You will need to give your User ID and password as a security check before your bid can be registered.

Confirmation of Your Bid

If you are ahead of the field, a page appears that confirms your bid has been accepted and you are the high bidder.

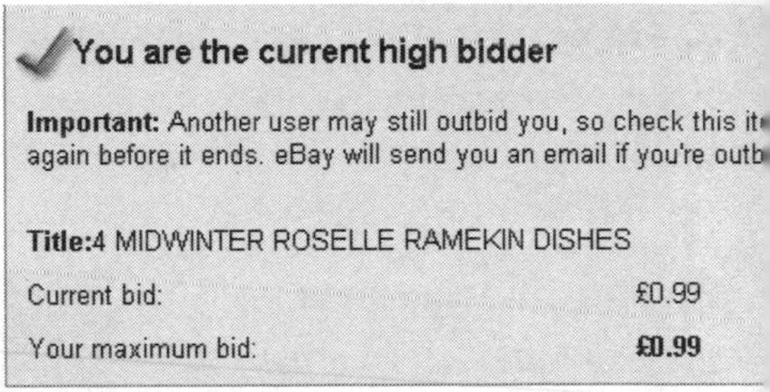

You are the current high bidder

Important: Another user may still outbid you, so check this it again before it ends. eBay will send you an email if you're outb

Title:4 MIDWINTER ROSELLE RAMEKIN DISHES

Current bid: £0.99

Your maximum bid: **£0.99**

You will also receive an email from eBay confirming that you have placed a bid.

bidconfirm@ebay... eBay Bid Confirmed: 4 MIDWINTER ROSELLE

However, if another keen bidder has placed a proxy bid, (explained below), you are not the high bidder and a screen like the one below will appear. You have the option to place a higher bid or look around for something else.

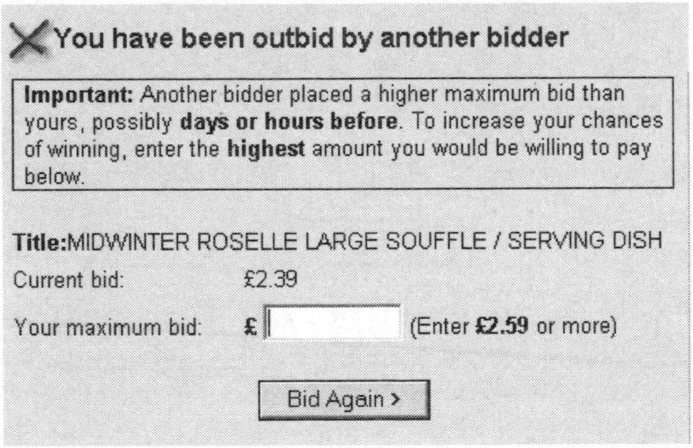

You have been outbid by another bidder

Important: Another bidder placed a higher maximum bid than yours, possibly **days or hours before**. To increase your chances of winning, enter the **highest** amount you would be willing to pay below.

Title:MIDWINTER ROSELLE LARGE SOUFFLE / SERVING DISH

Current bid: £2.39

Your maximum bid: £ (Enter **£2.59** or more)

Bid Again >

Email from eBay

If you are the high bidder you will remain so until another bidder leaves a bigger bid. If at any stage you are outbid by another trader, you will receive an email to let you know.

At the end of the auction you will be sent an email saying you have won the item.

on@eba eBay Item Won! Marilyn Monroe - My V

If you are outbid in the final days or minutes an email will arrive, like the one below, with the disappointing news. However, this news is sweetened with a selection of similar items and, in the event of the money burning a hole in your pocket, you can dry your tears and take a look.

fitem@ebay.... eBay - Item Not Won, Similar Items Found: Midwint

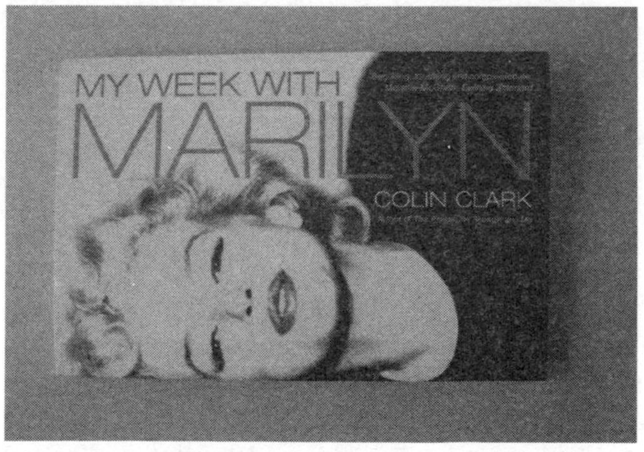

Bidding on Reserve Price Auctions

Starting bid **£10.00 (Reserve not met)**

Place Bid >

Some sellers put reserves on their items. This means that they set a reserve price somewhere above the start price below which they are not obliged to sell. The rules changed some time ago and the lowest reserve price possible is £50.

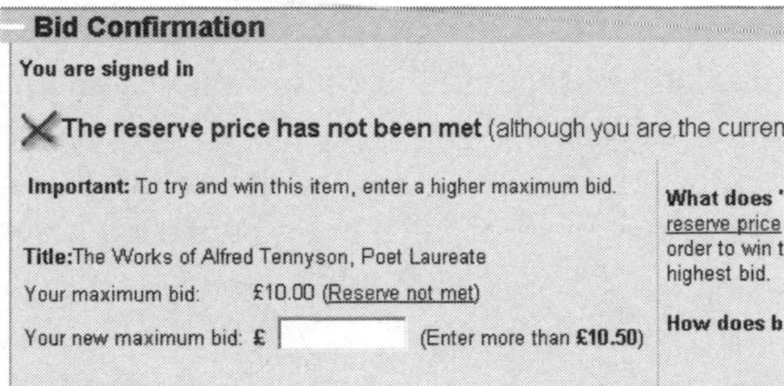

They could, of course, select a higher start price instead of setting a reserve but many sellers believe that a low start price attracts interest. The reserve price is not shared with the bidders and browsers but once the eBay bidding reaches the reserve the notice changes to **Reserve met.**

In the example above the start price for The Works of Alfred Tennyson was set at £10. A bid was placed for £20 but did not meet the reserve. Even if this turned out to be the only bid it would fail to secure the book.

eBay auctions without reserves are attractive to buyers. Some eBay entrepreneurs operate a very exciting trading policy and start all their auctions at £0.99 with no reserve. It ensures their auctions have a wide following and their insertion costs are low, but it must take nerves of steel!

Bidding by Proxy

Alternatively, you can opt to use the proxy system, which allows you to put in the highest sum that you would be prepared to pay for that item, and eBay automatically ups your bid as other buyers increase theirs.

How Bidding by Proxy Works

Let's say that you want to buy the Troika vase that you have found. The seller sets the opening price at £40 and there is no reserve. You are prepared to pay £350 and put this sum into the bidding facility. You are the immediate high bidder and the auction price is shown as £40. However, a few days into the auction another Troika collector puts in a proxy bid of £75. The auction immediately jumps up to the next increment, say £80, with you as the high bidder. If no-one else places a bid you win the item at £80. However, if in the final day of the auction someone places a bid of £360, they are the final high bidder and win the vase.

The Advantages of Bidding by Proxy

You will not get carried away and place a higher bid than you originally intended

If away from home the system bids in your absence

You only bid enough to win the item, up to your limit.

The Disadvantages of Bidding by Proxy

You declare your hand at an early point and can easily be outbid.

Early proxy bids are believed to raise the price of an item because buyers have time to re-assess their bidding levels and raise the stakes.

You miss out on the excitement of the final moments.

Sniping

This is the eBay expression for placing a bid in the final minutes or even seconds of an auction. Many buyers believe they get the best deal by waiting until the very end to register their interest and it makes the auctions very exciting for both buyers and sellers. Much of their success comes down to timing, which has to be very precise, and the speed of their internet connection. However, I would not recommend that beginners enter this last minute fray until they are completely confident of their abilities. I have received telephone calls from anxious students who have inadvertently placed bids with the decimal point in the wrong place! These matters were easy to put right with the luxury of time, but as last-minute bids they could have been very distressing and costly.

You Have Won the Item

When the auction has come to a close and you are the high bidder, you will receive an email from eBay informing you of the good news.

. eBay Item Won! BRAVEMOUTH, Living with Billy Connolly by P. Stephensor

You need to get cracking as there are several things you must do to complete your side of the transaction.

As the Auction Winner you need to:

- Make contact with the seller asap
- Agree the final price including cost of shipping
- State how you intend to pay
- Make payment promptly.

You Are the High Bidder!

Make It Snappy! The next few days are critical to making a good impression and you should act promptly. Do not place bids if you are going on holiday or are too busy to make payment within a few days after your win.

Make contact with the seller. You can do this using the email that eBay send informing you that you have won the item, or you can initiate contact via **My eBay.** It is also likely that the seller will contact you by sending an email invoice. All offer easy links for payment.

Agree the final price. You need to ensure payment covers costs of shipping (the postage, packing and any insurance charges) to the final price. Bear in mind that if you had bought the item from an auction house you would incur travel and transport costs.

State how you intend to pay. If they offer several payment options, and you have no preferences, you might like to ask what they prefer. This is nice and friendly and sets the tone of your transaction. Bear in mind if you pay via PayPal it costs you nothing, but the seller is charged a small fee. However, some sellers prefer PayPal because it is instant and secure. Chapter 5 covers how to make payments using PayPal.

How to Pay by Cheque

Many sellers send their buyers an invoice to assist payment. It looks like the email below.

aw-confirm@ebay... Your invoice for eBay purchases - item #69095223

Open up the invoice email which gives the item number.

Here is the invoice for your item,

This invoice gives the financial details of the transaction including price and shipping charges. If there were any additional costs or discounts, these too would be listed here. In the example below the cost of the book is £1.20 and postage and packing, £2.70. This gives a total of £3.90. This is the sum that needs to be sent to the seller.

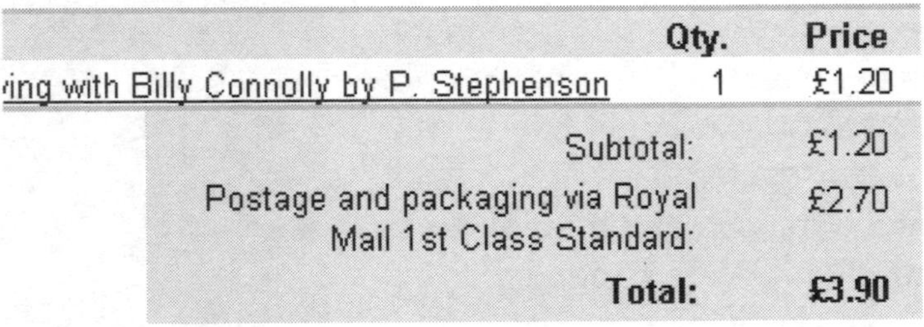

	Qty.	Price
ving with Billy Connolly by P. Stephenson	1	£1.20
	Subtotal:	£1.20
	Postage and packaging via Royal Mail 1st Class Standard:	£2.70
	Total:	**£3.90**

The name and address of the seller appears at the bottom left-hand side of the invoice.

It is advisable to send a copy of the invoice with your cheque to help the seller identify the payment.

Communicating Direct with the Seller

Alternatively, you can email the seller and ask for payment details.

Receiving the Item & Finishing the Deal

When you pay by cheque, as opposed to PayPal, you will almost certainly have to wait longer for your item to arrive.

- The cheque needs to reach its destination
- Allow time for your seller to bank your cheque
- The cheque needs to clear
- The item takes time to reach you.

Checking the Item

When the item arrives you should check straight away that it is as described. Most eBay transactions go well and the buyers are happy with the goods. If you are not satisfied with your item you should get back to your seller and communicate how it does not match up to the description. Most hitches are resolved with tact and diplomacy. If you are content with your item you should post feedback as described in Chapter 4.

Leaving Feedback

Go to My eBay link located in the top row of home page.

My Account
- Personal Information
- Addresses
- Preferences
- Feedback
- PayPal Account

At the left-hand side of My eBay you will find **My Account.** Scan down to Feedback. This link will take you to the feedback forum where there is a space specifically for comments about this transaction. Write something nice.

excellent, friendly, service - recommended

8 Bidding & Paying

9. Preparing to Sell

Getting Organised

You need to get organised from the outset:

1. Auction Preparation Form

There are several decisions you need to make for each item you intend to sell and these are best done in advance of going online. You can type up a simple form containing all the points you need to address when creating your auction. This will act as a prompt and offer an opportunity to think it through.

2. Packaging Supplies

You will need to gather up or buy appropriate packaging materials. If you are not able to recycle all you require they can be bought locally, by mail order or online from suppliers such as Viking Direct.

3. Information on Postal Costs & Services

Take a trip to your local Post Office and pick up the comprehensive leaflets concerning postal costs within the United Kingdom and abroad. You should also ask about the cost and range of insurance services.

4. Get Yourself a Routine.

If you intend to sell regularly on eBay you would be wise to get yourself a routine. For instance, you could take and upload digital images on Fridays, prepare the descriptions on Saturdays, create your auctions on Sundays and pack and ship on Mondays. Most big sellers break the operation down into smaller tasks for particular days. Some even state in their auctions 'I ship on Tuesdays and Fridays', so that their buyers know exactly what is going on.

AUCTION PREPARATION FORM

Item
Measurements
Category/ sub-category
Title
Description
Start Price (Required)
Reserve Price (Optional)
Buy It Now Price (Optional)
Quantity (Qualifying Sellers)
Duration
Start Time (End Time)
Picture/s – File name & location- Size
Gallery option
Theme
Selling enhancements
Counter
Payment methods
Postage cost
Post-to locations

Useful Aids to Describing Condition:

Tape measure
Torch
Magnifying glass

To complete the sale:

File for paperwork
Packaging
Visit local Post office or purchase postal scales
Recorded delivery slips – get a supply from Post Office
Postal service receipt
Certificate of Posting

Item

You can sell most moral and legal items on eBay, though there are some restrictions. You can discover what is not allowed by going to Site Map.

Measurements

It is important to provide dimensions of the item (inches & centimetres if possible). When items are particularly heavy or light it is a good idea to include the weight.

Choosing a Category

One of the most critical decisions is determining the category / sub-category. Some buyers browse through the categories and so your item needs to be where they would expect it. For many items there is an obvious category whilst for others it takes a bit of detective work.

For example, suppose you want to sell this 1960s postal order, but are not sure about the category. A quick way forward is to undertake a key word search for postal orders so that you can discover their categories. If they are all in the same category this is where your postal order needs to be. If the search reveals a variety of categories you need to examine the auctions to find the most appropriate for your type of postal order. Two of these refer to 'Billy Bunter' books and can be discounted.

Coins (4)
- Banknotes (4)

Books, Comics & Magazines (2)
- Children's Books (2)

Collectables (1)
- Paper & Ephemera (1)

Stamps (1)

The best category for the postal order is probably:
Coins / BankNotes / British / English / Elizabeth II

Toying With a Title

Your title is limited to 55 characters (with no asterisks or quotes) and is the first impression of your auction. You need to ensure that you make the most of it.

Key Words

It is very important that your title contains the key words associated with the item. Many buyers search using key words and you should ensure that your title contains the most obvious in relation to the item. You need to think laterally around the topic and draw upon the words that your buyers might use in their search. You should make the inclusion of key words a priority over and above the way the title reads.

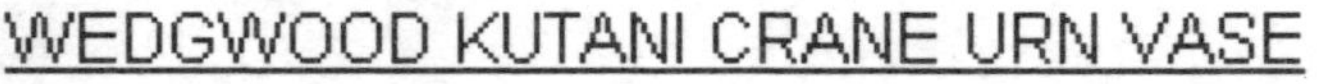

WEDGWOOD KUTANI CRANE URN VASE

Stating Exactly What It Is

You should state exactly what your item is, even if the title repeats the category, and include the brand name, designer or artist.

Stunning Black Patent Leather ,Vintage 40's Shoes!

Only use words like 'stunning' and 'delightful' when you have used up all the critical key words. However, such endorsements are worthwhile when you have the space.

Researching the Winning Titles

Sort by: Price: highest first

You can look at Completed Items and Sort by: Price highest first, to examine the titles of the most successful auctions in your category.

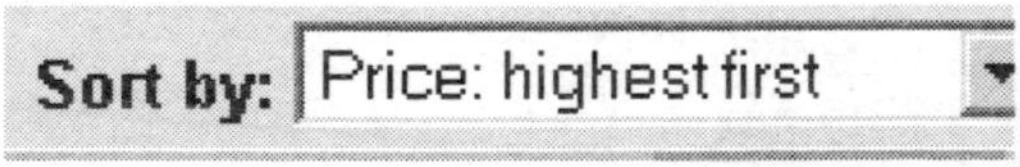

Describing Condition

One of the most challenging aspects of creating your auction is describing condition. If your item is in perfect condition it is more straightforward. However, 'perfect' is a big claim and you should not assume that because something is new that it is necessarily pristine. It is important to look everything over very carefully. Even if you have owned something for years you need to examine it with fresh eyes.

If the item is nearly new, antique or collectable you need to describe it thoroughly and with care. You have to bear in mind that your buyer cannot handle and examine the item for themselves and so you have to do it for them and write it all down. You must point out chips, cracks, tears, flaws, rubbing and wear. If the damage is slight you should mention it and then dismiss it, for example:

- 'There is a teeny scratch on the underside of the saucer, but it is hardly noticeable.'
- 'The finish on the wooden lid is a little worn but it does not detract.'

It is important to be enthusiastic about your item and stress the good, but this must be tempered with the stark realities about its condition.

.

3-Point Plan for Describing Condition

- Start off enthusiastically with the selling points
- Move on to cover dimensions and condition
- Finish with a reminder about the charm, etc.

Useful expressions when describing condition are

.....in good condition for age......

.....no real damage but a little tired.....

.....some slight rubbing........

.....absolutely minuscule......

Whenever possible include:

New Items

If it is the latest and most up to date model
Special features
Information on guarantee or warranty
Details of accessories or upgrades.

Antique or Collectable Items

History is always a plus point
Family connections add fascination
Proof of provenance makes an item more desirable
Information about marks and signatures
Point out possible uses
Always draw attention to a No Reserve price auction.

Example of Description

Delightful Victorian Glass Pickle Jar NR

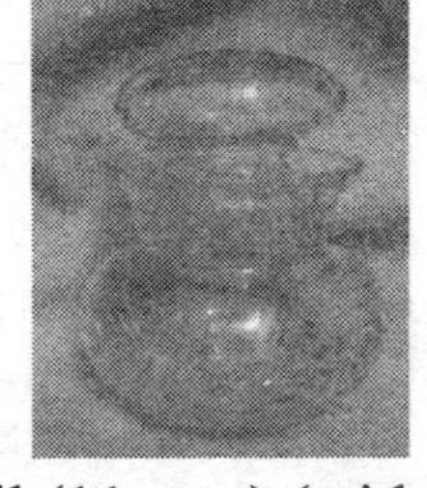

This is a lovely, and increasingly hard to find, vintage glass pickle jar made in the mid to late nineteenth century, before the days of freezers when preserving fruit and vegetables was a part of everyday life.
The storage jar was hand blown and the geometric pattern around the bowl was hand cut. The jar stands about 4.5inches tall (11 cms) (with glass stopper) and measures 3.5 inches (9 cms) at its widest point. The rim is 2.5 inches (6 cms) in diameter. It is a quality item and fairly heavy. It is in good condition for its age though not perfect. There is a small chip in the rim. There are some slight wear marks on the base which are part and parcel of its great age. It is attractive, useful and a part of English history. It would look equally good in the kitchen or bathroom. There is no reserve so the first bid could win it!

Start Price

This is the opening price below which bids do not register. Clearly the lower the start price the more likely you are to attract bids. Some sellers have a policy of starting everything off at rock bottom prices. However, you have to bear in mind that the first bid might turn out to be only bid and, providing you have not placed a reserve, you are legally bound to sell the item. Your insertion fee is based upon the start price (providing there is no reserve price). A start price is not optional.

Buy It Now price

Qualifying sellers can choose to place a BIN price. This means that the buyer can by-pass the auction process and opt to pay the indicated price for an instant purchase.

£13.99 Buy It Now

Quantity

Qualifying sellers can sell multiple items.

Duration

Do you want your auction to last 1, 3, 5, 7 or 10 days? There is no difference in cost and clearly a longer auction will be seen by more potential buyers. You need to bear in mind when you want it to end and work back from there. It is widely believed that auctions that end on weekend afternoons achieve better final prices than those that end mid-week, when most people are at work.

Consider Your Market

You also need to give some thought to your main market. If you are selling Susie Cooper wares, which are popular in Japan, it is probably best to close on the Japanese equivalent of a Sunday afternoon. However, there is an ongoing debate about the optimum time span and some sellers believe that buyers lose interest in a 10-day auction.

Start Time

You can delay the start, and therefore end, of your auction to your best advantage. See previous paragraph.

Pictures

Note on your form the file names and location of the pictures you intend to use, e.g. My Pictures, eBay Selling, Wedgwood Striker.

Wedgwood Striker

There are many options regarding pictures. Do not skimp on pictures, they can make or break a sale.

Gallery Option

This is a very cost-effective auction feature.

Theme

There are many different themes to choose from.

Selling Enhancements

Your choice of selling enhancements will depend on the nature and value of the item you are selling. These are entirely optional.

Counter

These are very useful to gauge interest.

Payment Options

You must state how you like to receive payment and it is a good idea to offer as wide a choice as possible. Bear in mind just one additional bidder will raise the price.

- PayPal is wonderful for attracting foreign buyers, though you will find many UK buyers prefer it too
- You might want to stipulate that you will also accept personal cheques from United Kingdom to cater for individuals who do not accept PayPal.

Postage Costs
It is advisable to discover these before you create your auction as buyers like to know where they stand in relation to additional costs. Alternately you could weigh the item, give the postal costs within the UK and state that you are happy to quote shipping costs to foreign lands. This saves you having to quote lots of different prices each time.

Post-to Locations
You must decide whether to sell just within the UK or worldwide. You can also select which countries you will post to.

Friendly Note

You may want to create a compliments slip to accompany your item, thanking your buyer for their custom and politely reminding them to leave feedback. If you offer an attractive trading policy such as 'no quibble refund if my description is wrong' you should mention it on this slip. In the event of your item not coming up to scratch your buyer is aware that the problem will be resolved.

Free Listing Days!

At regular intervals eBay hold days where you can list your items free of charge. Sometimes they apply to one particular feature, e.g. free listing for items that offer PayPal as a payment option. These special days are a great incentive to sellers and you should ensure that you are prepared with pictures and descriptions to take full advantage. Please note that the listing aspect of the charge is free but you will be charged the final value fee as usual.

9 Preparing to Sell

10. Pictures

The Importance of Pictures

Strictly speaking you do not need to use pictures to sell things on eBay but you are highly unlikely to achieve your best price without them. The first picture is part of the package, and so it is advisable to use at least one. However additional pictures cost just 12p each and represent the best value sales enhancement available as they can be enormously powerful when it comes to tempting buyers and giving them confidence. Also, if some minor damage is mentioned in the description of an item, a close-up of the hairline crack will put buyers' minds at rest by confirming just how slight it is.

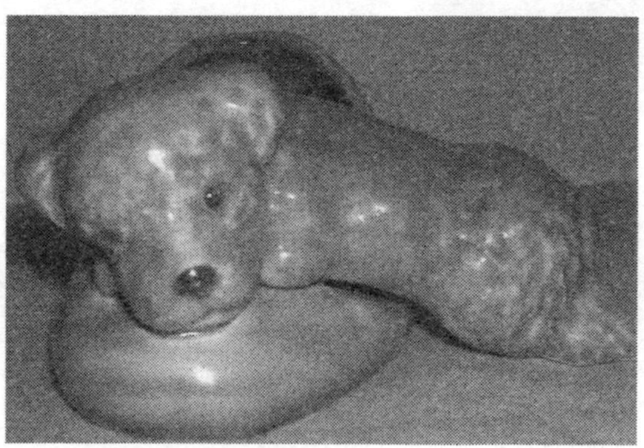

eBay requires digital images. These are easily created with a digital camera or scanner and are uploaded onto your computer. When you create your auction you insert the pictures by the click of a mouse.

Uses for pictures

- Use a picture to show the overall look
- Different angles give further information
- Special features can be highlighted
- Close-up of delightful details
- Marks and signatures can be flaunted
- Wear, tear and damage is fairly shown
- Receipts, guarantees and manuals can make the sale.

A picture of this lovely coffee can and saucer made by the Derby factory in the early nineteenth century can persuade buyers in a way that words never could.

Pictures tap into the emotions and speak straight to the heart.

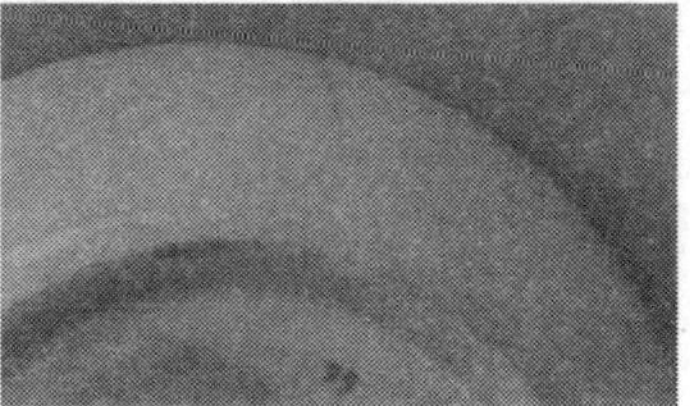

Buyers are wary of damage but a picture illustrating exactly how it looks can put their minds at rest.

Marks are a big selling point when it comes to auctions of antiques and collectables and this fine Derby mark and painter's mark would undoubtedly ensure a sale.

If possible it is a good idea to show how the mark sits in relation to the item as a whole.

The additional marks on the underside of this cup are signs of age and as such should be flaunted.

This mid twentieth century mahogany radio box had been in the wars! It has sustained a fair amount of water damage as well as scratches and such things could put off buyers.

However the inclusion of the wonderful BBC mark gave it increased fascination and secured a buyer. In my opinion it was the mark that clinched the sale.

Digital Images

Many people already own a digital camera and will be aware of just how easy and convenient they are to use. They differ from conventional cameras in that they record images in a memory, rather than on film, and it is this feature that makes them so practical and versatile. When you take a picture with your digital camera you can view it immediately and if it is not exactly what you want you can delete it and take another. Digital cameras are ideal for eBay sellers and if you do not already own one, it is probably worthwhile splashing out.

There are a fantastic number of different makes of digital camera and they vary enormously in price from £30 to thousands. This subject is too vast and specialised to cover in this guide but when choosing a camera the important thing to consider is the longer term. It is often said that the minimal quality required by screen pictures allows you to get away with buying an extremely cheap camera. In my experience it is wisest to spend at least £100 on a well-known make of digital camera in order to allow you to show off your items to their best. If you already own a digital camera you will be able to adapt the settings for the kind of image that is suitable for an eBay auction.

Some digital cameras are supplied with rechargeable batteries and a charger and this should be added to the list of considerations when weighing up price. If you buy a digital camera with standard batteries it might be advisable to invest in rechargeable batteries and a battery charger which are much more cost effective and convenient.

A New Digital Camera

If buying a new digital camera you need to connect it to your computer. Your package is likely to include:

Digital Camera

The software on a CD

A USB cable – (check provided)

An instruction manual

Possibly a quick start guide.

First you need to install the software onto your computer. You need to turn your computer on and place the software CD into the drive of your computer. This automatically starts up a series of instructions that can be easily followed. You will then be ready to take and store pictures of the items you want to sell.

Next you need to locate the USB port on your computer. This can be slightly tricky to find and it is a good idea to satisfy yourself that you know where it is. I have known cases of computers not having these, but this is fairly rare. The absence of a spare USB port can be easily remedied by fitting a multi-port hub; this simply requires making contact with your friendly PC supplier.

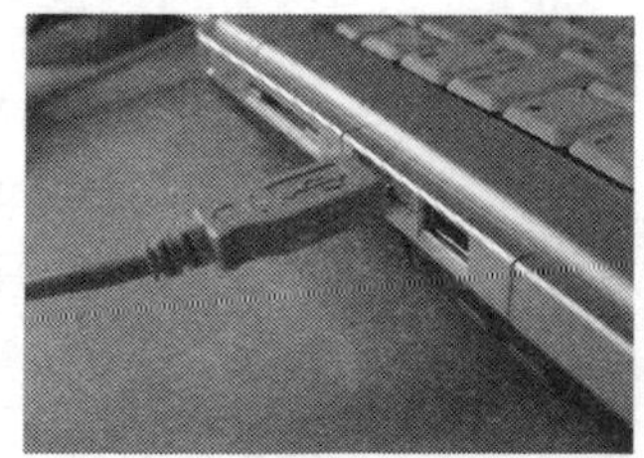

Background & Lighting

It is amazing what small things make or break a sale and it is important to give some thought to the background. If you are likely to sell items of a similar size it may be possible to set up a small permanent 'studio' with a fabric background that enables you to take pictures quickly and easily.

A fixed studio set-up would also enable you to perfect the lighting which can make a great deal of difference to the end result. However, if you are simply seeking a one-off shot, good effective lighting is achieved outside, in the shade, on a reasonably bright day.

It is also possible to alter the settings on your camera to secure a good shot. You could take a look at the operating manual to determine the possibilities.

Finally, when you are really getting into your stride, you can invest in some editing software such as Adobe Photoshop Elements or Jasc Paint Shop Pro to enable you to manipulate and enhance your images.

However, millions of eBay sellers enjoy a great deal of success by taking simple shots with digital cameras by doing the following:

- Create a simple setting
- Alter the camera setting for the right size image
- Avoid using the flash
- Take numerous pictures at different angles
- View the pictures as you go and delete and re-take
- Upload your pictures into your eBay file
- Give each picture a name that easily identifies it.

Size Counts – the Right Size of Digital Image

The most critical aspect to success with your eBay pictures is the size of the digital image, which is quite different from that required for portrait or family shots and you will need to alter your camera settings to comply.

eBay images need to be small. For the purposes of selling on eBay they really need to be less than 100KB. Images that are larger than this take too long to upload into an auction and they will likely be rejected. The smaller the image the quicker the process and increased likelihood of success. It is possible to take a large size of image and make it smaller by editing it using computer tools but it is much simpler to take them small from the outset. It just takes a few seconds to alter the settings and saves fiddling around on your PC.

There are a wide variety of digital cameras but they all operate using the same basic principles. The step by step instructions that follow are for a Nikon Coolpix 3100 and illustrate how easy digital cameras are to use. You need to consult your instruction manual for the precise method for your camera.

Overview of Changing the Image Size Setting of a Nikon Coolpix 3100

To alter the setting to take small pictures you need to:

- Turn your camera on
- Switch the dial to taking picture mode
- Bring up the menu
- Select picture size
- Highlight the smallest option and select
- Press menu again to lose the menu.

Your camera is now ready to take pictures of a small enough size to sell items on eBay.

Step by Step Guide to Changing the Image Size Setting

Turn Your Camera On

Your on/off switch will be clearly marked on your camera and pointed out in your manual.

Switch the Dial to Picture Taking Mode

Most digital cameras have different modes and to alter the image size you have to select the picture taking mode as indicated in the picture.

Bring Up the Menu

The menu button will be clearly marked and when pressed it will show a list of choices on the LCD screen.

Select Picture Size

You should choose image size or image size/quality by moving the highlighter with the up and down arrows.

A number of choices will appear – High, Normal, PC Screen, TV screen. Select the smallest.

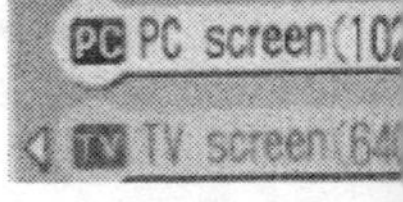

Press Menu Button

Press the menu button again and the screen will return to picture taking mode. You are ready to take small size images.

Taking Pictures

The good thing about requiring images of a small size is that you can fit a great number into your camera before the memory card is full. This means that you can experiment and take lots of pictures from different angles and select the ones that come out best.

Loading Your Pictures into Your Computer

You are now ready to transfer your pictures from your camera into your computer, taking care to place them in your especially prepared eBay selling file.

10 Steps to Uploading Pictures into the computer

1. Check you have opened an eBay selling file in Pictures
2. Plug the USB cable into the USB port in your computer
3. Plug the other end of the cable into your camera
4. Turn your camera on
5. Press transfer button or switch dial to transfer mode
6. This introduces a wizard onto your computer screen
7. Follow the instructions for uploading pictures
8. Ensure you store them in your eBay selling file
9. Give each picture file a name that identifies it
10. Turn off your camera and unplug the USB cable.

Checking the Size of Digital Images

Before you create your auction you should make certain that the images that you intend to use are the right size, i.e. not too large. This is easily done and just takes a minute.

- Locate the images in your eBay Selling file
- Rest the cursor on the image
- A window appears giving information about the picture
- It includes: Dimensions, Date Picture Taken, Cameral Model, Type, and Size in KB. The size needs to be under 100KB.

The size of the Melon Dish to the right is 726KB. This is too big to load into an eBay auction.

The size of the Lamb image is just 75.3KB and will work well in my auction.

11. Creating Your Auction

Policy for new sellers

It is a good idea for new sellers to have first experienced buying on eBay as this gives them a feel for the process and they get to understand what it is like to be on the other side of the counter. I would also recommend that your first few sales are restricted to the UK as it is more straightforward. You are best advised to select an item of modest value and keep your real money-spinners for when you are entirely confident and can make the most of this global opportunity.

Checklist for Selling

You have an item to sell

You have taken digital pictures

The pictures are stored on your computer

You know where they are and the file name

You have examined the item carefully and noted damage

You have thought of a title containing the key words

You have written an enthusiastic but accurate description

You have decided on the category

You have considered a start price

You have determined postal costs.

14 Steps to Creating Your Auction

In order to create your auction you need to complete the selling form which takes you through the various options.

1. Click on to the Sell at the top of the home page. (At this point you need to give your ID and password)

Buy	Sell	My eBay	Community	Help

2. Select **Online Auction** by positioning the cursor in the circle and clicking the mouse. Click **Sell Your Item.**

How would you like to sell your item?

(•) Online Auction - Allow bidding or offer a Buy it Now price.

( ) Fixed Price - Let buyers purchase your item at a set price.

Sell Your Item >

Sell on online Auctions – An auction is created to last 1, 3, 7, or 10 days, depending on what suits and with no difference in cost to the seller. The item is sold to the high bidder at the end of the auction.

Sell at a Fixed Price – In fixed price auctions items are offered for a number of days at a fixed price. There is no bidding as items are purchased instantly and the auction is cut short by the successful sale.

3. Choose your Category

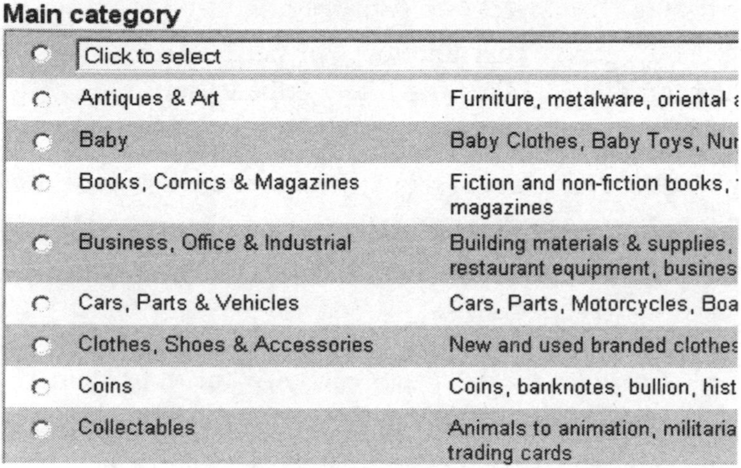

Main category

○	Click to select	
○	Antiques & Art	Furniture, metalware, oriental a
○	Baby	Baby Clothes, Baby Toys, Nur
○	Books, Comics & Magazines	Fiction and non-fiction books, magazines
○	Business, Office & Industrial	Building materials & supplies, restaurant equipment, busines
○	Cars, Parts & Vehicles	Cars, Parts, Motorcycles, Boa
○	Clothes, Shoes & Accessories	New and used branded clothes
○	Coins	Coins, banknotes, bullion, hist
○	Collectables	Animals to animation, militaria trading cards

- Make your selection from the list provided.

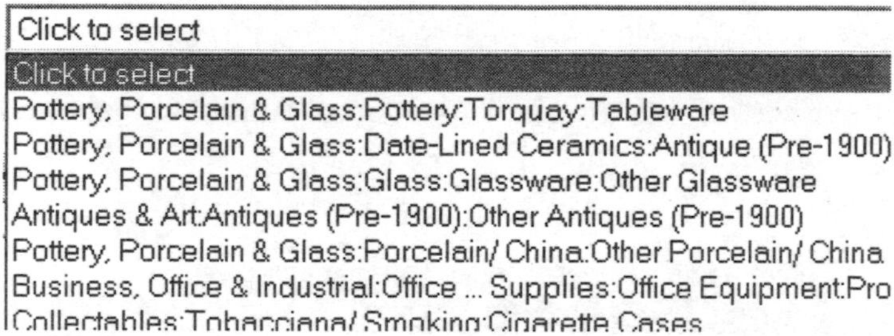

Click to select

Click to select
Pottery, Porcelain & Glass:Pottery:Torquay:Tableware
Pottery, Porcelain & Glass:Date-Lined Ceramics:Antique (Pre-1900)
Pottery, Porcelain & Glass:Glass:Glassware:Other Glassware
Antiques & Art:Antiques (Pre-1900):Other Antiques (Pre-1900)
Pottery, Porcelain & Glass:Porcelain/ China:Other Porcelain/ China
Business, Office & Industrial:Office ... Supplies:Office Equipment:Pro
Collectables:Tobacciana/ Smoking:Cigarette Cases

- You have the option to choose a second category
- A second category increases visibility and cost
- A second category is good for high value items
- In this instance, for the sake of simplicity we will not select it
- Take the cursor to the bottom of the page
- Select Continue.

< Back   Continue >

4. Choose Your Sub Category

1. Collectables

To change the top-level category, click the **Back** button below.

2.
- Advertising ->
- Animals ->
- Animation ->
- Autographs ->
- Badges/ Patches ->
- Bottles/ Pots ->
- Breweriana ->
- Casino ->
- Cigarette/ Tea/ Gum Cards ->

3.
- Milk
- Miniatures
- Perfume
- Poison
- Whiskey
- Wine/ Black Glass
- Cream/ Preserve Pots
- Pot Lids/ Ointment Pots
- Other Bottles/ Pots

- Consider the best sub category for your item and select it
- You can find the best category using a key word search

Main category # 13909

- You will be allocated a category number as above
- Use it for similar items to save time

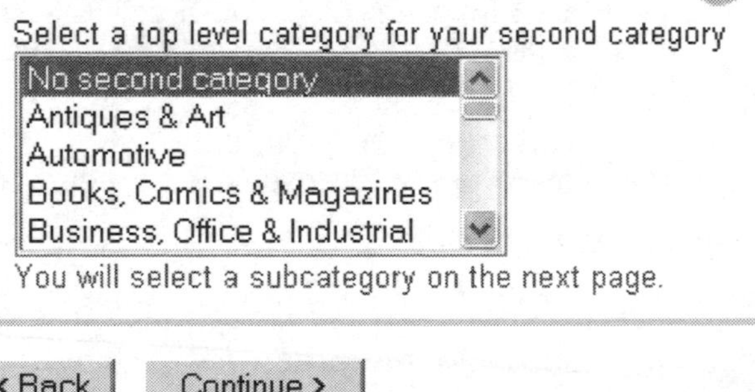

- Select **No second category** and click **Continue.**

5. Enter Your Title

Sell Your Item: Describe Your Item

1. Category **2 Title & Description** 3. Pictures & Details

Item title *Required

Hand Made Old English Green Glass Wine Bottle c 1750

3 characters left; no HTML, asterisks, or quotes.
Ensure your title contains specific details about your item.

- Type your title in the space provided
- Your title should contain the main key words (see Chapter 9 – Preparing to Sell).

6. Enter Your Description

Item description *

Describe your items features, benefits, and condition. Make s
and dimensions or size. You may also want to include notabl
Black Glass.

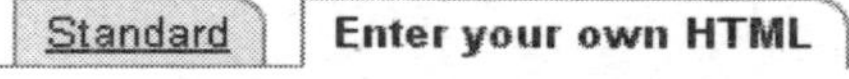

NEW! Select Inserts from the drop-down list below to quickly

This is a rare and exciting wine bottle. Its dumpy shape ind
middle of the eighteenth century. Wine bottles that precede
those that came later became more cylindrical to assist sto

- Type your description containing key words
- Vary spelling: 18th century and eighteenth century
- Be enthusiastic but accurate
- All damage, however slight, should be mentioned
- Give dimensions.

7. Auction Sale Details

Pricing and duration

Starting price * Required

£ 2.60

Bidding will begin at your starting price.

Buy It Now price (£0.06)

£

Sell to the first buyer who meets your Buy It Now price.

- Enter your start price
- Qualifying buyers can add a **Buy It Now Price**
- **Buy It Now** shortcuts the auction process for keen buyers

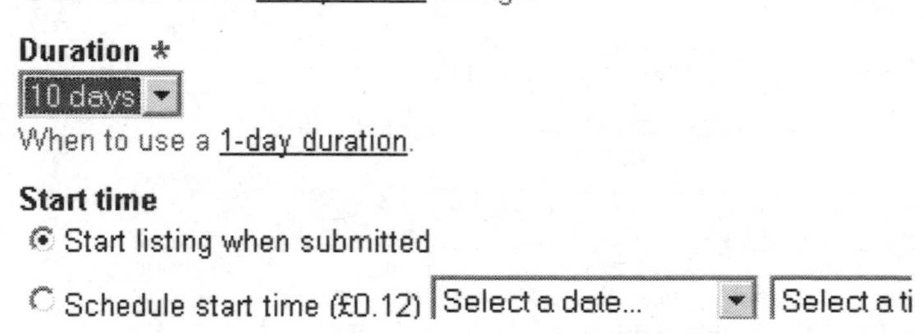

- This auction is for one item-multiples are possible
- How many days you want it to last? This is for 10
- There is a charge of 12p to defer the auction start
- This auction will start straight away
- Location – check that your location details are correct.

8. Adding Pictures

Picture 1 (Free)

Browse...

To add pictures to your listing, click Browse.

Picture 2 (£0.12)

Browse...

Picture 3 (£0.12)

Browse...

Picture 4 (£0.12)

Browse...

- Position cursor over **Browse** of Picture 1 – click mouse

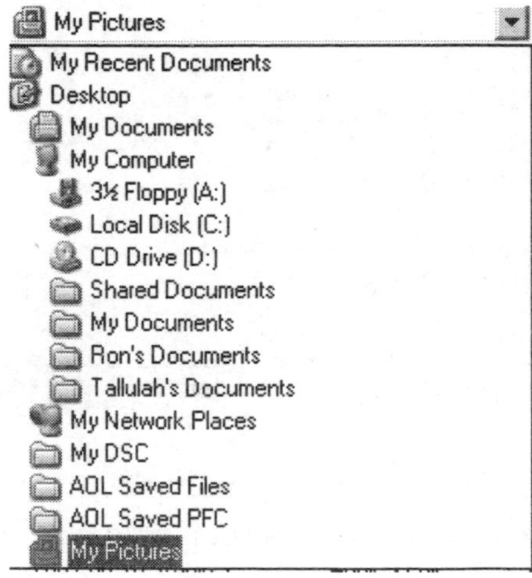

- This allows you to locate the **My Pictures** file
- From there you can find your **eBay selling** file

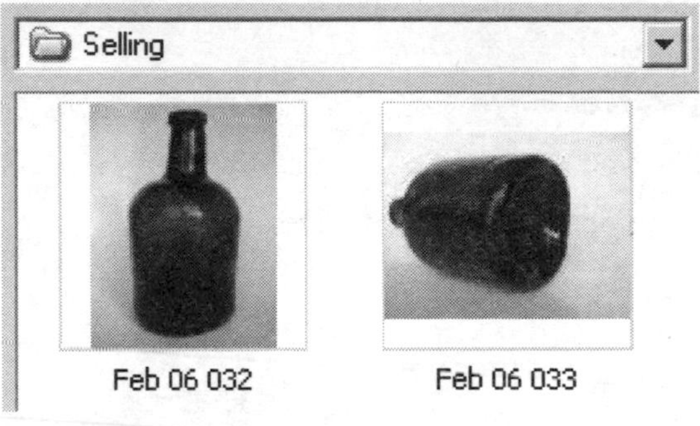

- Find the picture you have chosen for this auction
- Click on it to incorporate it into your auction
- To add more pictures continue the process
- Take the cursor to **Browse** on Picture 2 and click
- It returns to the pictures in your eBay selling file

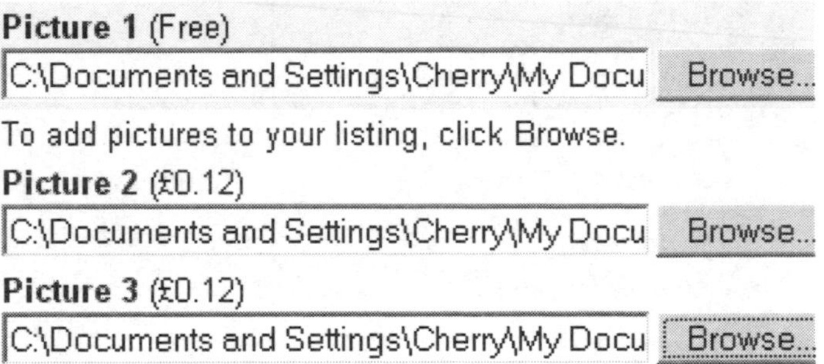

- When pictures are added the section looks like this
- You can choose to add up to 6 pictures in all
- You do not need to use all 6
- There is a de-select option if you make a mistake.

9. Selling Enhancements

- There are several exciting selling enhancements
- The costly one is Home Page Featured - £49.95
- The least expensive ones are Designer Theme – 7p, Gallery – 15p and additional pictures – 12p
- For beginners selling a modest item the best are:

Gallery options
Applies to first picture
☑ Gallery (£0.15)
Add a small version of your first picture to se

- The gallery adds a thumbnail picture for browsers
- At a cost of just 15p it is excellent value

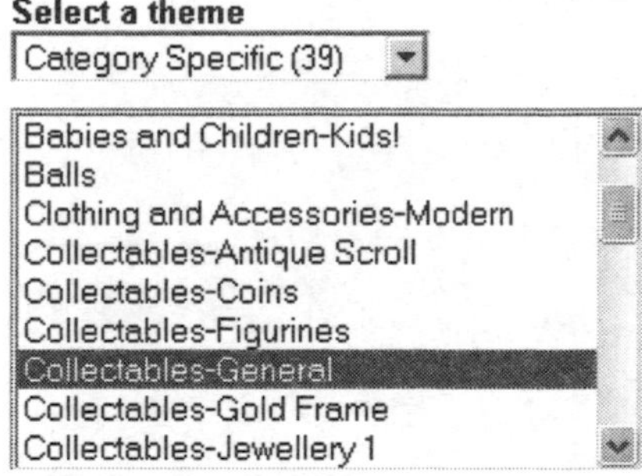

- Themes are fun and brighten up your auction
- They are inexpensive and easy to use
- Page counters gauge interest and are free.

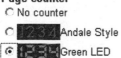

Page counter
○ No counter
○ 1234 Andale Style
◉ 1234 Green LED

10. Loading Pictures

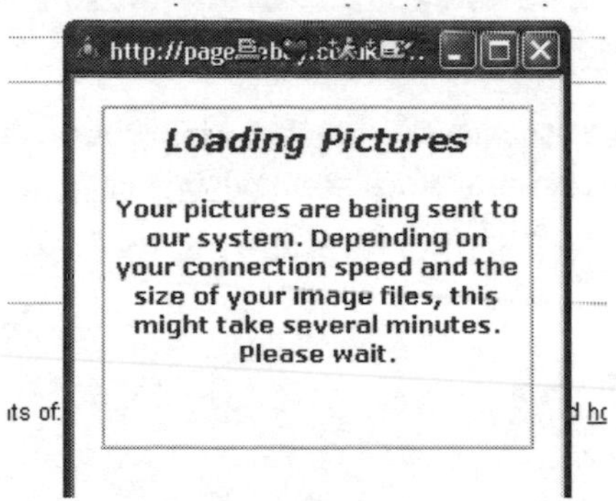

- It takes a few minutes to load your pictures
- Large will not work.

11. Payment & Postage

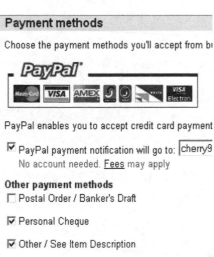

- How you will accept payment?
- The more options you give the more sellers you attract
- PayPal is the most attractive payment option for overseas buyers.

Payment methods

Choose the payment methods you'll accept from bı

PayPal enables you to accept credit card payment

☑ PayPal payment notification will go to: cherry9
No account needed. Fees may apply

Other payment methods

☐ Postal Order / Banker's Draft

☑ Personal Cheque

☑ Other / See Item Description

☐ Credit Cards

12. Where in the World?

Post-to locations *Required

(•) Will post to United Kingdom and the following (check all that ap
Reach more buyers - learn more about posting internationally.
☐ Worldwide ☐ N. and S. America ☐ Europe
☐ United States ☐ European Uni
☐ Canada ☐ Ireland
☐ France
☐ Germany

( ) Will not post - local pickup only

- Select where you will post the item
- Beginners are advised to start within the UK
- You could achieve a higher price by trading globally

Postage *

Specify a flat cost for each postal service you offer.

Domestic Postage (offer up to 3 services)
Royal Mail 1st Class Standard (1 to 2 working days) ▾ £ 5.50

- You can give postage costs in the auction details
- Buyers are then in no doubt as to the final cost
- Using this option gives buyers confidence to bid
- Postage information encourages late bidders
- Insurance is optional but you can state your policy
- Enter your Payment instructions and return policy.

13. Review Your Listing

Step 1: Review your listing

Preview how your item will look to buyers

Click an 'Edit page' link to make changes. When you do, yc

Title

Hand Made Old English Green Glass Wine Bottle c 1750

- All aspects of your auction can be changed by clicking on to the appropriate edit
- It takes you back into the text to alter it

Edit title

Edit subtitle

Edit description

Edit Pictures

- Changes can be incorporated with **Save Amendment**
- Pictures can be altered just as easily as the text
- Click on edit to return to the picture selection link

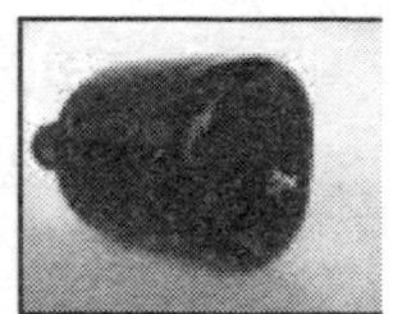

Duration:	10 days
Quantity:	1
Price:	**£14.90**
Item Location:	Highbridge, United Kingdom
Listing Designer:	Theme: Dining Out Layout: Standard
Listing Upgrades:	Gallery

- Ensure your details are correct
- Check on the options and selling enhancements
- It is very easy to return to amend any detail

Step 2: Review the fees and submit your listing

Listing fees (Incl. VAT)	
Insertion fee:	£ 0.35
Additional pictures:	0.24
Gallery:	0.15
Listing Designer:	0.07
Total added listing fees: *	**£ 0.81**

- Check on the fees before you go any further
- All charges are broken down and easy to understand
- Selling costs comprise a listing fee and final value fee
- Final value fees only apply when the item sells
- Placing an item in two categories doubles the listing fee (but not the final value fee).

14. Submit Listing

-

< Back | Submit Listing

Your item will be listed on eBay and the above fees

- When you have checked the details click **Submit Listing**
- You will be informed of a successful listing
- If not you will be asked for missing information
- You will receive an email in confirmation.

listingconfirm@e... eBay Listing Confirmed: Fine En

- The email confirms the details of your auction.

12. Watching Your Auction

My eBay

You need to keep an eye on your auction and a very convenient way to do this is through My eBay. My eBay contains everything on the site that specifically concerns you. It lists the items that you are selling, watching, and bidding on. It contains a section with your account details and preferences, as well as a range of other very useful options.

My Summary

All Buying
- Watching (6)
- Bidding
- Best Offers
- Won (7)
- Didn't Win (4)
- My Recommendati

All Selling
- Scheduled
- Selling (1)
- Sold (10)

My eBay is particularly useful when it comes to keeping track of the items that you are selling as it gives you the state of the poll for each and is a reminder of what you need to do. It tells you the current price, how much time is left on an auction and how many bids have been placed. It even lets you know how many people are watching your auction and so gives an indication of the interest in your item. Even though the Large Pine Cupboard (below) has not yet received a bid there are 10 watchers. Many buyers wait until the closing minutes before placing a bid.

Current Price	Bids	High Bidder ID	# of Watchers	# of Questions
Large Old Victorian Pitch Pine School Storage Cupboard				
£49.90	0	--	10	2

Checking Emails

You need to check your emails regularly when your auctions are in progress in case a potential buyer has a query about the item. Welcome these enquiries as they are an opportunity to break the ice between you and your potential buyer. The speed and tone of your response could be critical to the decision to place a bid. There is something very reassuring about a seller who replies promptly and courteously to questions. If you did not state the cost of shipping in the auction details it is likely that a browser will get in touch about that. Alternatively, a nervous buyer might be concerned to clarify something in the description or want to make certain about the condition. A delay in responding to a question could mean that a bid is not placed and you will fail to achieve the best price. In the worst case scenario a delay in responding to a buyer's query could mean that your item fails to sell.

Assessing the Response

You should check that your auction is attracting attention. To do this you can visit the auction page and scan down until you come to the Counter. This is a Smart Counter and logs the number of unique viewers. So, if a keen potential buyer visits your auction twenty times, it will only register on the counter once. It is a great help in determining the profile of your auction and how successful it has been in attracting browsers. If the counter indicates there have been few visitors you have an opportunity to add selling enhancements and raise the profile of your auction. It is very easy to amend an auction while it is in progress, although some restrictions apply.

History of the Bidding

The auction page itself offers a great deal of information about the ongoing sale. It gives the location of the item, the duration of the auction and the time the auction still has to run. It also shows the current bid price and the user name of the high bidder along with their feedback rating. However, of more practical use is the history of the bidding which is revealed by using the number of bids link. By clicking on this link you can investigate the active bidders and note their feedback scores.

User ID:	Bid Amount	Date of bid
nina_ste (1593 ★)	£17.89	25-May-06 C
gas (600 ★)	£16.89	19-May-06 1

Second Chance Offer

In the event of your high bidder pulling out of the sale it is possible to make a Second Chance Offer to a non-winning bidder at the bidder's maximum bid amount. (Sellers should not resort to this lightly but try to resolve things with the high bidder first). To initiate this process you should go to My eBay / Sold / Bid History / Second Chance Offer. Please note that Second Chance Offers will only go to bidders who have opted to receive them, go to My eBay / My Account / Preferences / Notification Preferences.

sha_dog (549 ★) Send Second Chance Offer	£78.00
reen_teddy (78 ★) Send Second Chance Offer	£51.00

Revising a Live Auction

If you think that your auction is not attracting sufficient attention or interest you can enhance it whilst it is on-going. There is also a possibility that another eBay member will contact you about the item you are selling offering information that would be good to include in the description. Changes are easy to make and can make a significant difference to the final outcome. There are many things you can do, including:

- Change the category
- Add a second category
- Change or add pictures
- Add promotional features, bold or highlight
- Add a gallery picture
- Change the title
- Change the description
- Lower the start price.

Restrictions to Revising Your Auction

Providing your auction has received no bids and does not end within 12 hours, you can:

- Revise anything in your listing except the selling format (it must remain as an auction)

If your item has received bids or ends within 12 hours you can only:

- Add to the item description
- Add optional seller features to increase visibility.

(If your item has received a bid AND ends within 12 hours you cannot add to the description or add a second category)

How to Revise Your Auction

Locate your item in My eBay.

Access the auction page by positioning the cursor and clicking on the title.

Quality - Old English Custard or Jelly Glass c 1820

£4.80
Buy It Now £16.00 0 -- C

You are now in your auction page and can assess what needs to be changed.

Making Changes to Your Auction

Revise your item
Promote your item
Sell a similar item

Go to the top of the auction page to find the links that make it easy to revise aspects of your auction.

These links take you back to the original auction form where you can decide on additional promotional features, or change / add pictures.

Having made the changes you need to save them by clicking the link at the bottom of the page.

Please Note – In the event of a description being revised the bidders are entitled to withdraw their bids.

Promote Your Item

If you select Promote your item you will be taken through the steps that allow you to choose additional promotional options. You will, of course, be charged for these. You should check that the item number is listed in the box and press Continue to proceed.

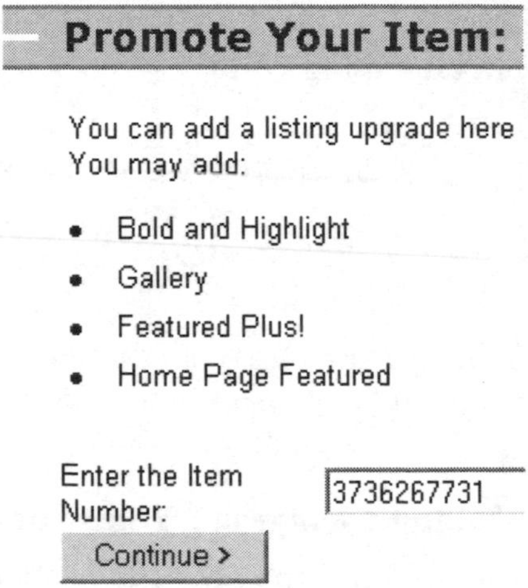

Revise Your Item

If you select Revise Your Item, you will start the process to change details in your auction. You might want to lower the start price, remove the reserve, change the title or description.

You can alter your auction by clicking onto the Edit links at the right-hand side of this page. It is similar to the editing option when creating your auction. You must save the changes at the bottom of the page.

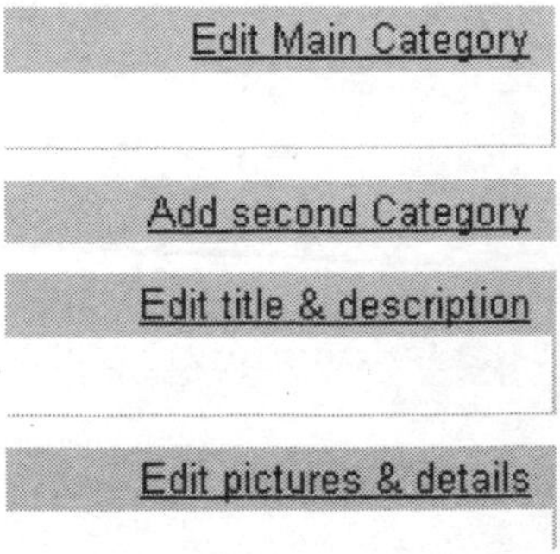

Adding and Changing Pictures

There is no doubt that pictures are critical to gaining the best possible price for an item. In this auction of an old jelly glass it seems likely that the poor quality of the picture is putting buyers off. It is easy to change:

- Note location of the replacement picture
- Go to **My eBay**
- Click on the jelly glass auction
- Select **Revise my item**
- Scan down to and select **Edit pictures**
- Choose the picture you want to replace
- Select Delete existing picture, as below
- Click on Browse and find replacement picture
- Select replacement picture.

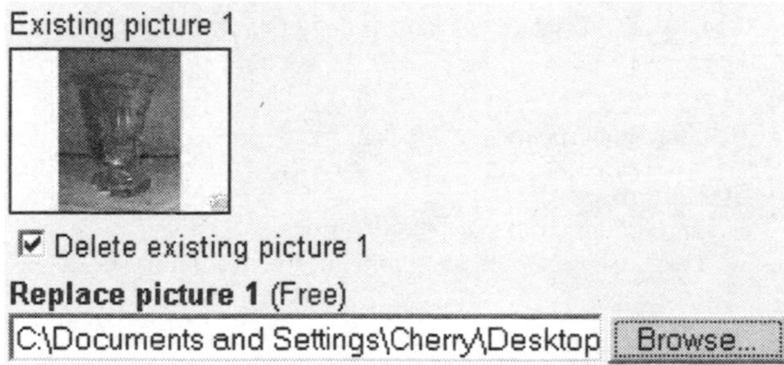

Here is the revised picture. It took just minutes to change and is far more attractive to buyers.

Re-Listing Your Item

If your item fails to sell, help is at hand. You can re-list it straight away by using the links. It is a good idea to consider why it failed to sell and think about incorporating changes to make it more attractive to buyers. There is a Relist link in My eBay (shown below on right-hand side).

English Cup & Saucer

-- 0 11-Jul Relist

This takes you into the auction listing page with the edit links. The process to re-list is similar to that of reviewing and editing your original auction.

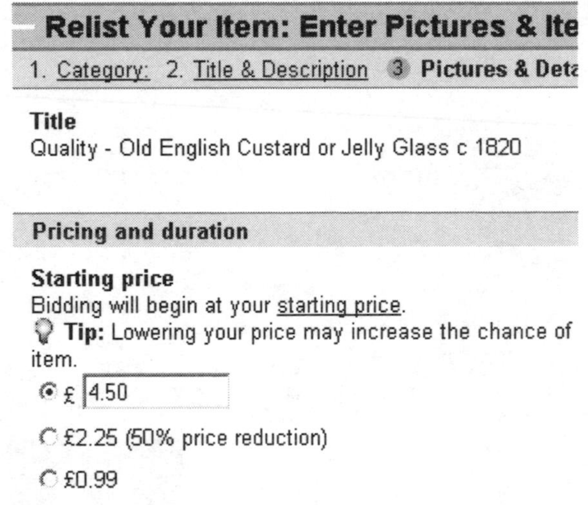

Charges

You will only be charged to re-list your item if it fails to sell again. This is an incentive to thinking it through and making changes to your title, description or start price.

Congratulations – Your Item Has Sold

You will receive an email from eBay informing you of the sale. You need to make prompt and friendly contact with your buyer.

endofauction@eba eBay - Item Purchase: 3M Model 2770 Port...

Shipping Costs

If you have stated cost of shipping in your auction you can send your buyer an email or invoice (an easy format using a link on auction page) giving total cost.

If not, you should ask where your buyer is located, discover the cost of shipping and send an invoice.

When looking into the postal cost of an item make sure that you weigh the item with all the packaging you intend to use. Just the additional brown paper can make a significant difference to the cost when sending an item abroad.

Sending an Invoice

It is very easy to send an invoice. Go to My eBay, to the summary of things sold and locate the item. On the right-hand side of the page is the Send Invoice Link, as below.

ıat	Qty	Sale Price	Total Price	Sale Date ▽	Action
	1	£5.50	--	20-Jul	Send Invoice

ı Custard or Jelly Glass c 1820 (3736267731)

This brings up an invoice format which you can adapt by adding insurance charges if appropriate. You also have an opportunity to send the buyer a message. You select Submit at the bottom of the page and your buyer is automatically sent their invoice. The status of the sale in My eBay changes to 'Awaiting Payment'.

Receiving Payment

If your buyer pays by PayPal you will receive an email confirming the transaction. The advantage of PayPal is that it is instant and you can receive payment instantly and send the item straight away. You should ship the item as soon as possible to ensure good feedback.

If your buyer pays by cheque you need to bank it and wait for it to clear before sending the item. This is good practice and entirely acceptable. Buyers who opt to pay by cheque must expect this delay, though the seller should progress things as quickly as possible. It is a good idea to email your buyer when you receive the cheque to put their mind at rest and to keep them informed, and sweet.

Packing the Item

After the effort of listing and selling the item you need to ensure that you wrap it carefully. It is your responsibility to ensure that it is properly wrapped and will stand up to the rigours of the postal service. You need:

- Sturdy boxes
- Padded envelopes
- Bubble wrap
- Newspaper.

I Only Charge Actual Postage

You can often spot an eBay trader as they eye up the empty boxes. It is a good idea to recycle packaging and gather up freebies as this allows you to limit your shipping charges to postage only. Buyers hate the idea that they are being overcharged for shipping and it is a big selling point to state in your auction details that you only charge actual postage.

Choice of Postal & Delivery Services

There are a range of postal services including:

Royal Mail / Royal Mail Special Delivery (www.royalmail.com) and Parcel Force (www.parcelforce.com)

There are private delivery services that specialize in eBay deliveries. www.getitmoved.co.uk is a low-cost delivery service. Have all details, such as addresses, etc., to hand.

You need to consider which is most appropriate for your item and much will depend on its nature and value. In terms of security it is wisest to use postal services that track the progress of a package to its destination.

Offering Insurance

Much depends on the value of the item. Clearly it would be foolish to send some items without insurance, but for everyday low-cost items many traders do not bother. Bear in mind that there is some slight insurance factor within the cost of regular posting. However, insurance is an important matter and a personal choice. For parcels moving within the United Kingdom it can be a good idea to send it Recorded Delivery. This currently costs very little and means that the item has to be signed for when it arrives at its destination.

Another option is to operate your own insurance scheme. You can add a small sum to the cost of shipping in case of problems. If an item is lost or damaged in transit you simply return the payment. The theory is that the sum built up covers the occasional loss. It is vital that you indicate the cost of shipping and state that it includes insurance. It is a gamble but saves the bother of putting in a claim in the event of loss or damage.

Proof of Posting

Whatever you and your buyer decide, it is essential that you ask for a Certificate of Posting and keep it safe with the rest of the paperwork relating to this item. In the event of a dispute you will need to supply proof of posting.

Leaving Feedback

It is always good to learn that the item arrived safely and your buyer is pleased. They will either email you to let you know, or simply leave feedback. As the seller you too should leave feedback and, providing things went well, you need to say something generous that reflects the nature of the transaction. You can start this process from My eBay.

Outside Offers

When an item fails to sell you might receive an email from an eBay member asking to buy it privately. Do not be tempted to do this, it is against eBay's rules and such transactions are not covered by the protection schemes.

Do not underestimate our postal service! It took two of us to carry these (3 ft x 2 ft approx) pine shelves, to our local Post Office but they were sent to Nottingham for under £15.00. The delighted buyer gave me wonderful feedback!

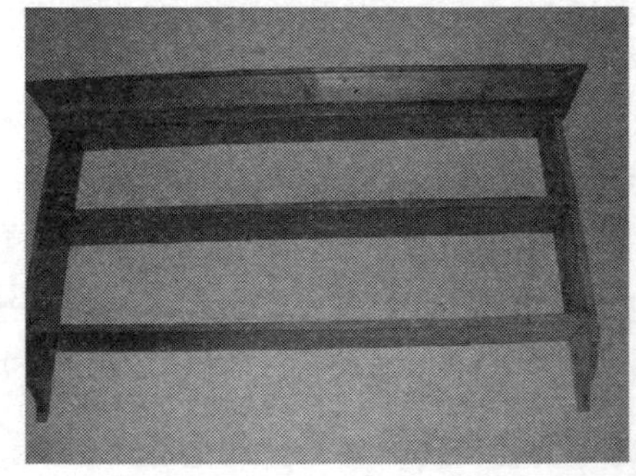

13. Fees & Accounts

The Cost of Trading on eBay

Browsing and buying on eBay is free but sellers are charged a small fee (very approximately 5%) to list and sell items. The fee is composed of two parts:

- **Listing Fee** – non refundable
- **Final Value Fee** – only applies if item sells.

Listing Fee

The listing fee is comprised of the insertion fee plus optional extras, such as additional pictures. The listing fee is charged regardless of whether or not the item sells and varies according to the type of listing.

Summary of Fees Charged to eBay Sellers

Listing Fee + Final Value Fee (if item sells) = eBay Fees

Insertion Fee + Sellers Optional Extras = Listing Fee

Final Value Fee is a graded percentage of Selling Price.

Car & Real Estate Auction Fees are calculated differently and are not covered in this guide.

Value Added Tax

All fees quoted include VAT @ 17.5% for residents of the UK. If you are a business you can avoid VAT on your seller fees by entering your VAT registration when creating your business account. Go to Site Map / Registration / Business Registration.

The Insertion Fee

This is based on the start price or reserve price as follows: (The prices quoted are for auction style listings and do not include cars or real estate).

Opening Value or Reserve Price	Insertion Fee
£0.01 - £0.99	£0.15
£1.00 - £4.99	£0.20
£5.00 - £14.99	£0.35
£15.00 - £29.99	£0.75
£30.00 - £99.99	£1.50
£100.00 plus	£2.00

(In a **Reserve Price Listing**, the Insertion Fee is based on the reserve price for your item, not the opening value.)

(In a **Buy It Now Only** auction the Insertion Fee is based on the Buy It Now price for your item.)

Examples of insertion fees

If you create an auction for a collectable doll and give the start price as £0.50, the insertion fee will be £0.15.

If you create an auction for a book and give the start price as £7.00 with no reserve, the insertion fee is £0.35.

If you create an auction for a doll and give the start price as £20.00 the insertion fee will be £0.75.

If you create an auction for your old school tie and give the start price as £35.00, the insertion fee is £1.50.

If you create an auction for a pair of leather riding boots and give the start price as £180, the insertion fee is £2.00.

If you create an auction for an antique four-poster bed with a start price of £1,950, the insertion fee is £2.00.

Additional Reserve Price Insertion Fee

Reserve Price	Reserve Price Listing Fee
£0.01 - £49.99	N/A
£50.00 - £4,999.99	2%
£5,000.00 plus	£100.00

This fee only applies if the item fails to sell and is a way of keeping reserve prices realistic. The lowest possible reserve is £50.

Auction Style Multiple Item Insertion Fee

The Insertion Fee is based upon the opening value of the items you list multiplied by the quantity of items you offer. The highest such fee for a multiple item listing is £2.00.

Buy It Now Only Multiple Item Listing

The Insertion Fee is based upon the Buy It Now price of the items offered for sale. The start value is the Buy It Now price multiplied by the quantity of items you offer. The maximum insertion fee for any multiple item Buy It Now Only listing is £2.00.

Re-Listing Fees

If an item fails to sell the seller is encouraged to list it again with a view to making the auction more attractive to buyers. For example you can add pictures or improve the title or description. Re-listing fees only apply if the item fails to sell. If the seller successfully sells the second time around he or she is only charged for one set of listing fees, plus the final value fee.

Examples: Insertion, Buy It Now & Reserve Price Fees

The example below shows the listing fee for an auction with a start price of £0.50 and a Buy It Now price of £50.00. The level of BIN makes no difference to the insertion fee because there is no reserve and the item could sell for £0.50. (BIN fees vary from 5p to 25p)

Listing fees (Incl. VAT)	
Insertion fee:	£ 0.15
Buy It Now Fee:	0.25
Total added listing fees: *	**£ 0.40**

In the example below the item has been listed with a start price of £0.50 and a reserve price of £50.00. The reserve price takes the insertion fee to £1.50. It incurs a Reserve Price Auction fee of £1.00 but is refunded if the item sells.

Listing fees (Incl. VAT)	
Insertion fee:	£ 1.50
Reserve Price Listing:	1.00
Total added listing fees: *	**£ 2.50**

In the example below the start price of £50 puts the insertion fee up to £1.50 and the BIN price of £100.00 sets the BIN fee at £0.25.

Listing fees (Incl. VAT)	
Insertion fee:	£ 1.50
Buy It Now Fee:	0.25
Total added listing fees: *	**£ 1.75**

Final Value Fee

The final value is the closing bid. You will not be charged a Final Value Fee if there were no bids or if the item fails to reach the reserve.

On Buy It Now auctions the final value is the Buy It Now price. There is no final value fee if the item fails to sell.

Final Value Fees

The charges are graded as follows:

5.25% of the amount of the winning bid or Buy It Now price up to £29.99.

3.25% of the amount of the winning bid or Buy It Now price from £30.00 to £599.99.

1.75% of the remaining winning bid or Buy It Now price greater than £600.00.

Examples of Final Value Fees

If an item sells for £15.00 the Final Value Fee is £0.79

If an item sells for £30.00 the Final Value Fee is £1.57

If an item sells for £151.00 the Final Value Fee is £5.50.

If an item sells for £1,500 the Final Value Fee is £49.35.

If item fails to reach its reserve there is no Final Value Fee.

Looking up eBay's Fees.

To check on all eBay's fees you can go to:

- Help
- Selling
- What are eBay's fees?

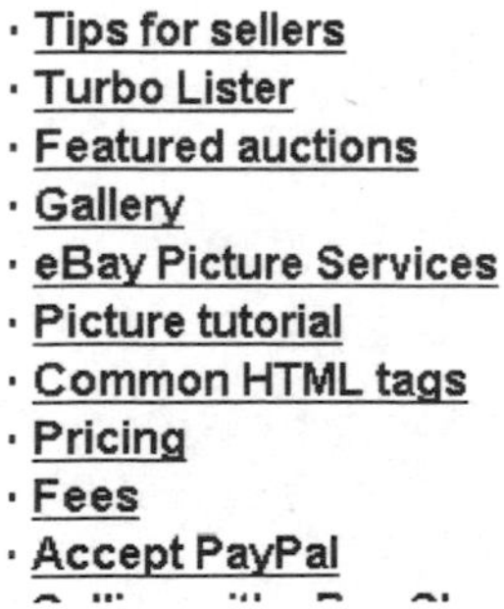

· Tips for sellers
· Turbo Lister
· Featured auctions
· Gallery
· eBay Picture Services
· Picture tutorial
· Common HTML tags
· Pricing
· Fees
· Accept PayPal

The Cost of Optional Auction Sale Enhancements

Scheduled Listing-£0.12

You can time the start (and therefore end) of your auction.

Additional Pictures-£0.12

In a standard auction you can include up to 6 pictures. The first picture is free.

Gallery-£0.15

This offers a thumbnail picture to accompany your listing.

TONI RAYMOND "flour shaker"

Gallery Featured-£15.95

Add a small version of your first picture to search and listings and include your picture in the Featured Area of the Gallery view.

Picture Options

Supersize pictures-£0.60

Slide Show-£0.60

Picture Pack-£0.90 or **£1.35**

Enhance Visibility

Listing Designer-£0.07

Bold-£0.75

Highlight-£2.50

Promote Listing

Features Plus-£9.95

Home Page Featured-£49.95

Reviewing Fees

In the process of creating your auction, but just before you submit it, you have an opportunity to review the charges. It is important to consider carefully your choices and ensure you are getting best value for money.

Examples of eBay Listing Fees

This auction below has a start price of £20 and a reserve price of £55. The £55 reserve price raises the insertion fee to £1.50. It also means that an additional fee of £1.10 applies, but this is refunded if the items sells. Two pictures (one free) incurs the cost of £0.12 picture fee. It includes the Gallery Featured at £15.95 and a promotional Highlight, £2.50.

Listing fees (Incl. VAT)	
Insertion fee:	£ 1.50
Reserve Price Listing:	1.10
Additional pictures:	0.12
Gallery Featured:	15.95
Highlight:	2.50
Total added listing fees: *	**£ 21.17**

Portable Overhead Projector

Sold for £150 – (£5.50)

Start price of £60 – (£1.50)

Four Pictures – (£0.36)

No reserve

Total eBay Fees-£7.36

Checking Your Account

It is very easy to check your account as the details are available 24 hours a day, 7 days a week.

You should go to My eBay (as a security check you will need to enter your password)

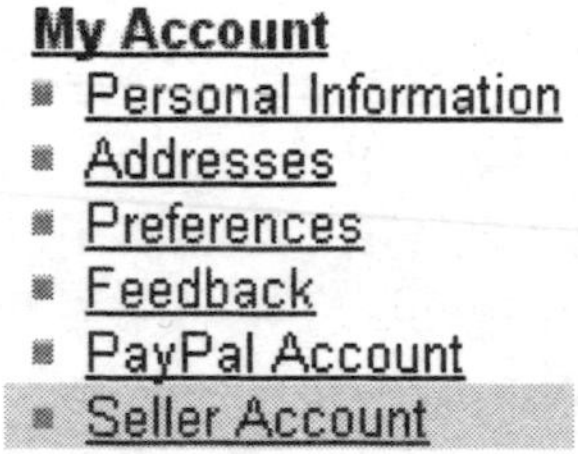

My Account
- Personal Information
- Addresses
- Preferences
- Feedback
- PayPal Account
- Seller Account

In the left-hand side of the opening My eBay page are various links, including the link to your account details.

Select **Seller Account**.

This takes you to the opening page of your eBay account. You can choose to see your most recent invoice or select **View Account Status** for more details, as shown below.

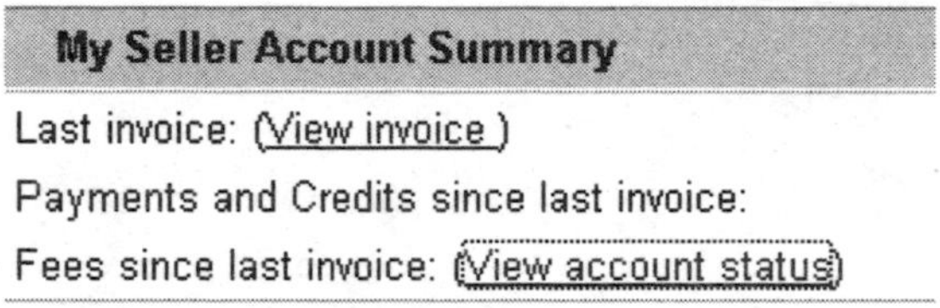

My Seller Account Summary

Last invoice: (View invoice)

Payments and Credits since last invoice:

Fees since last invoice: (View account status)

You can view past activity (up to 4 months at a time). Enter the appropriate dates and click on **View Account Status**.

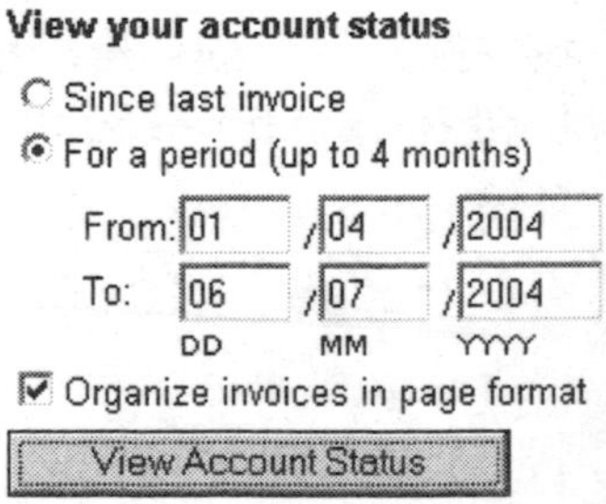

View your account status

Since last invoice

For a period (up to 4 months)

From: 01 / 04 / 2004

To: 06 / 07 / 2004

DD MM YYYY

Organize invoices in page format

View Account Status

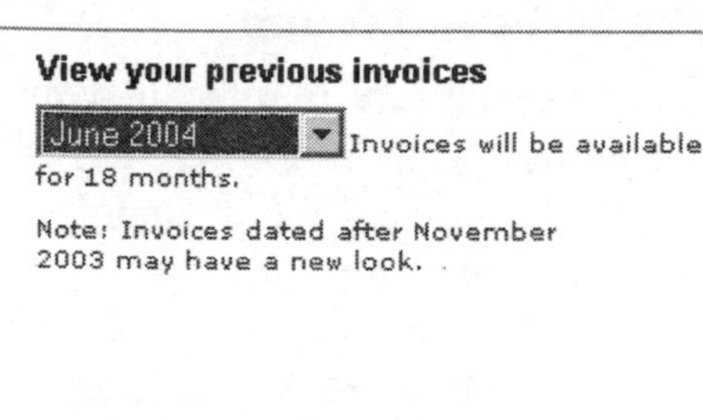
View your previous invoices
June 2004
Invoices will be available for 18 months.
Note: Invoices dated after November 2003 may have a new look.
View Selected Invoice

Alternatively, you can view your previous invoices. Click on the browser arrow to bring up the choices and select the desired month. The example shows June 2004.

Details of your sales are listed in date order and show the date, title, item number, type of charge (e.g. picture fee), VAT charged, fee and in the final column is the running total. It is simple to scan down and identify particular items, as shown below.

Derby Porcelain Coffee Can	3715737930	Picture Fee
Derby Porcelain Coffee Can	3715737930	Gallery Fee
Derby Porcelain Coffee Can	3715737930	Listing Designer Fee
Derby Porcelain Coffee Can	3715737930	Insertion Fee

The example below shows the insertion fee of £1.50, the Listing Designer Fee of £0.07. There is a Gallery Fee of £0.15 and picture fee of £0.24 (the auction included 3 pictures – first free and £0.24 for the others).

Insertion Fee	17.5%	£1.276596	£1.50
Listing Designer Fee	17.5%	£0.059574	£0.07
Gallery Fee	17.5%	£0.127660	£0.15
Picture Fee	17.5%	£0.204256	£0.24

Finding the Final Value Fee on Your Account

You will find the Final Value Fee clearly marked in your account details. In the example below the Final Value Fee is in the middle row and is £1.57. It raised the outstanding sum to £31.40 as show in the final column.

Insertion Fee	17.5%	£1.276596	£1.50	£29.47
Final Value Fee	17.5%	£1.338000	£1.57	£31.04
Picture Fee	17.5%	£0.306384	£0.36	£31.40

This small Torquay ware coffee pot sold for £12, the final value fee was £0.63.

This secondhand multi-gym sold for £70, the final value fee was £2.87.

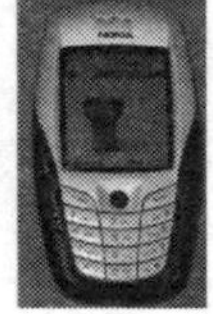

This nearly new Nokia 6600 Mobile Phone sold for £150, the final value fee was £5.47.

This new Vango Equinox 450 tent sold for £255, the final value fee was £8.89

This Dawes Galaxy Touring Bike sold for £350, the final value fee was £11.97.

Changing Your Account Details

It is very straightforward to change details of your eBay trading activity like your password or credit card. My eBay is a good start point for all changes that are personal to you.

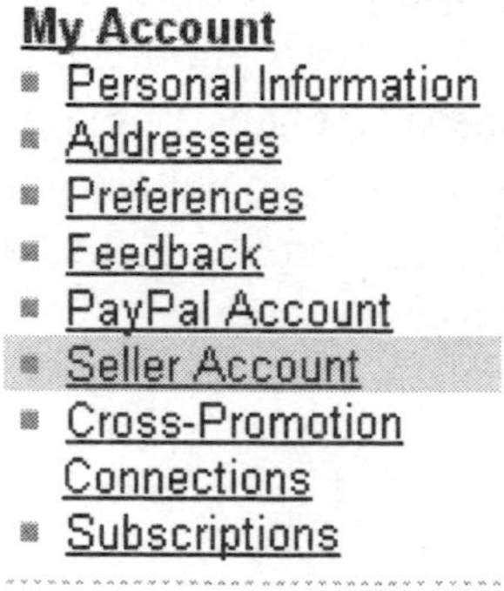

My Account
- Personal Information
- Addresses
- Preferences
- Feedback
- PayPal Account
- Seller Account
- Cross-Promotion Connections
- Subscriptions

You should go to the My Account section of your My eBay page and inspect the list of options.

The first two links allow you to keep your details current. The Preferences option allows you to tailor the notifications you receive from eBay to suit your exact requirements.

Personal Information

This section allows you to change things like your User ID, password or email address. It is here that you could also make changes to your billing and postal addresses. The page format offers:

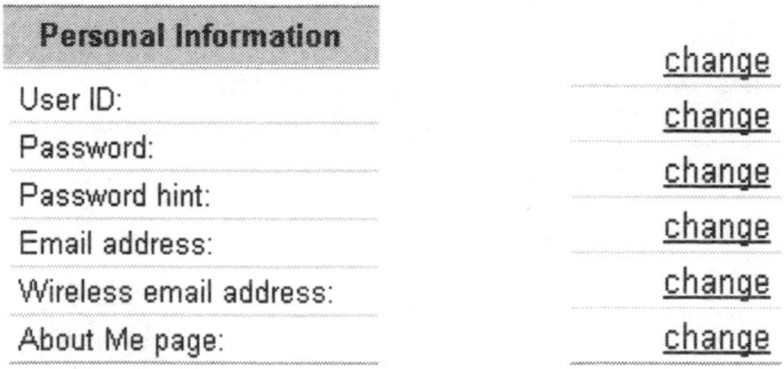

Personal Information	
User ID:	change
Password:	change
Password hint:	change
Email address:	change
Wireless email address:	change
About Me page:	change

Financial Information

Bank Account
Sort Code:
Account Number:

Credit Card
Card number:
Expiration date:

If you wanted to change your bank account or credit card you would use the appropriate link.

My Account

- Personal Information
- Addresses
- Preferences
- Feedback
- PayPal Account
- Seller Account
- Cross-Promotion Connections
- Subscriptions

In order to change your eBay preferences, for instance your notification preferences (for example, the emails you receive from eBay when you are no longer the high bidder), you should click on the eBay Preferences link. This takes you to a page that lists your current options and offers an opportunity to change them.

These include:

- Notification preferences
- eBay Sign In Preferences
- Seller Preferences (some of which are shown below)
- My eBay preferences.

Seller Preferences	
Sell Your Item picture preference:	**Basic eBay Picture Services**
Payment preferences	
Display Pay Now button:	**For all items**
PayPal Preferred:	**Off**
Offer PavPal on All Listinas:	**Yes**

Delivery preferences	
Offer combined payment discounts:	**Yes**
Unsuccessful bidder notices:	**Display both simila**
Participate in eBay merchandising:	**Yes**
VAT Status:	**Not Applied For**

14. Safety & Security

Why eBay is Safe

At the very top of the agenda for eBay is safety and security. Unfortunately internet crime is a feature of modern life and specialists in the eBay team work constantly to minimize the potential for the perpetrators. They have introduced a range of safeguards to protect both buyer and seller and it is wise to familiarize yourself with what is on offer:

- Encrypted Code
- Standard Buyer Protection
- PayPal Buyer Protection
- PayPal Seller Protection
- Escrow
- Square Trade
- Protection against Fraud
- My Messages.

Encrypted Code – eBay automatically encrypts the information you provide to keep it secure. It is stored on servers that are not directly connected to the internet; these are guarded both physically and electronically.Your information is not shared with other parties and enjoys the highest level of privacy that is currently available.

Standard Buyer Protection

This is the most fundamental protection offered to buyers and provides protection up to £120 (less £15 processing fee). It is most commonly called on when an item fails to arrive, or is significantly inferior to its description. It only comes into play when the seller has turned their back on their trading responsibilities or fails to communicate. Buyers must file a complaint within 90 days of the end of the auction. Buyers also need to check their eligibility, though the majority of traders will find that they are covered under this scheme. Standard Buyer Protection is not a substitute for postal insurance and does not cover goods that have been damaged in the post. Note:

- Compensation only covers the auction end price, not the total including postage and packing
- It covers the price, up to £120, minus £15 processing fee. For example a successful claim for an item that cost £85 is £70
- If your item was paid for with a credit card you should contact your credit card company first. If they fail to help you can file a claim, though you will need to prove they turned you down.

How to File a Claim

You need to assemble the following for your claim:

- The completed claim form
- A print-out of the auction listing
- Proof of payment – receipt, copy of cheque, etc.
- Copies of relevant emails and communications.

Go to: **Help / Transaction Problems / Protection for Buyers**

PayPal Buyer Protection

Buyers who opt to pay for their purchases with PayPal may well be eligible for compensation up to £500. PayPal investigate any claim and liaise with the buyer and seller to establish the facts surrounding the disputed transaction. The cover is for items that were paid for but not received or were significantly inferior to the description.

PayPal Buyer Protection Only Applies When:

- The auction listing displayed a PayPal Buyer Protection shield icon as shown below.

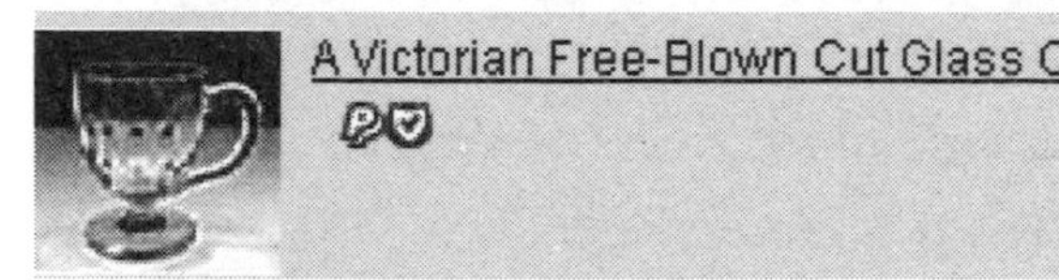

- The money was paid to the seller's email address associated with the listing. To ensure this you pay using the grey Pay Now button.

- The cover only applies to physical goods – services and intangibles are not included.

PayPal Buyer Protection Rules

- Buyers may only file one claim per payment
- Claims to be filed within 45 days of payment
- Buyers are limited to 3 PayPal refunds per year
- Information regarding the transaction must be provided.

Sellers Eligible to Offer PayPal Buyer Protection

PayPal's Buyer Protection is significant in terms of attracting buyers and new traders should work towards becoming eligible to offer it. Many buyers are inclined to limit their trading to auctions with this cover. They are aware that these sellers have a good track record and the chances of a happy outcome are extremely high.

PayPal Buyer Protection is offered by proven sellers:

- They have received 50 or more eBay feedback comments
- At least 98% of their feedback is positive
- They are verified members of PayPal
- Their account is in good standing.

PayPal Seller Protection

PayPal Seller Protection aims to protect sellers from losses arising from deceptive buyer activity. It covers situations where buyers falsely claim that goods did not arrive or cancel their credit card payment. Sellers without PayPal Seller Protection would be liable to make good the monetary losses plus the chargeback fees. However, eligible sellers are covered for up to £3,250 within one calendar year against such reversals. To be eligible sellers need to have a Premier or Business Account and comply with the UK Seller PayPal Protection conditions. These conditions include:

- The transaction concerns physical goods not services
- The goods were satisfactorily described.

Escrow

This is a safeguard whereby the payment for an item is sent to a neutral third party whilst the item is shipped to and examined by the buyer. When the buyer communicates to the escrow agent that the item is satisfactory, the payment is released to the seller, minus a small fee. Typically this is used for transactions involving large sums of money, though in reality it is a very affordable service. The first step in this process is for the buyer and seller to agree to use escrow and the exact terms, i.e. who pays for the service. eBay recommend www.escrow.com.

Square Trade

This is a service for eBay users that is designed to help resolve trading problems, Parts 1 – 3, below, are free.

1 - It rolls into action when a trader initiates the process by Filing a Case which involves completing a form (electronic) outlining the problem.

2 - The Square Trader contacts the other party and provides instruction on responding to the case. The case and all related responses are stored on a password-protected Case Page on the Square Trade website.

3 – Having outlined their ideas on the case, the buyer and seller discuss the matter in direct negotiation and try to reach an agreement.

4 - If direct negotiation fails to resolve the matter they can request a Square Trade Mediator to facilitate a solution. The mediator encourages the buyer and seller to solve the problem themselves and only recommends a solution if the parties request it. There is a charge for the mediator service.

Square Trade and Negative Feedback

It is very important to do everything you can to avoid negative feedback which, except for special circumstances, is permanent. Square Trade sometimes offers a way forward for removing it

A case must be filed outlining the problem after which Square Trade contacts the other party for their response.

If the other party assists a Square Trade Mediator is appointed to reach agreement and remove feedback

If the other party does not respond a Square Trade Reviewer is assigned to the case to investigate the possibility of removal.

Protection Against Fraud

eBay has an investigation team that looks into cases of reported fraud. They examine instances of alleged misconduct very carefully before coming to a conclusion and, if proven, disciplinary action varies from a formal warning to an outright ban from using the site. There are different kinds of offence that qualify for investigation but note that these do not include simple misunderstandings:

Feedback offences – including misusing the feedback forum to enhance their own reputation.

Bidding offences – including placing unwelcome bids in auctions where they have been barred.

Selling Offences – including using secondary IDs to artificially raise prices on their own auctions.

Identity offences – including representing themselves as eBay employees when they are not.

To report an offence go to **Help / Transaction Problems**

Buyer Beware List of Cautions

- Take time to check a seller's history and reputation
- If in doubt, email the seller and ask questions
- Avoid sellers who state a delayed delivery date – anything over 20 days after payment poses more risk
- PayPal sellers are not allowed to sell goods with delivery dates of over 20 days after payment
- Do not be tempted to trade outside of eBay – offers may be fraudulent and you have no protection
- In buying an antique or collectable, focus your attention to the seller and description as much as the picture.

My Messages

An ongoing problem on the site is the steady stream of 'phishing' emails. These fraudulent emails appear to be from eBay but are simply attempts to gain access to your user ID and password.

My Messages has been introduced to overcome this problem and will enable you to guarantee the authenticity of your messages. All eBay correspondence is duplicated in My Messages which is located in My eBay. It is easy and important to take a minute to ensure the message is valid.

Selling (4)
Sold (10)
Unsold (9)
Want It Now NEW!
My Messages (9)
All Favourites
Searches
Sellers
Categories

14 Safety & Security

15. When Things Go Wrong

An Overview of Solving Problems

Millions of transactions are completed on eBay every month without a hitch - these are rarely reported. The newsworthy stories are of the few that go wrong, though in reality they are few in percentage terms. With care most pitfalls can be avoided and small problems are usually sorted out amicably and with a bit of give and take.

eBay offers a service to help when things go wrong. It is unlikely that you will meet a problem that eBay personnel have not come across many times before and they are able to offer a way forward. You can always reach customer support by going to:

Help

Contact Us

(Located on the top left-hand side of any Help page.)

This brings up a form on which you can present your problem. You need to allow 24 – 72 hours for a response.

Problems & Solutions

You have placed a bid for £500 instead of £50.
If this occurs you should retract the bid immediately. You need to give the item number and choose one of the three reasons accepted for retracting a bid. In this instance select **Entered wrong bid amount.**

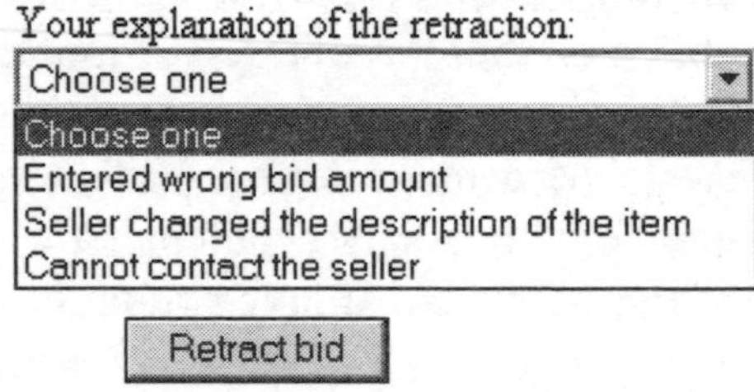
Your explanation of the retraction:
Choose one
Choose one
Entered wrong bid amount
Seller changed the description of the item
Cannot contact the seller
Retract bid

Your item fails to arrive
You should email your seller very politely giving details of the item including the item number. (Some sellers complete hundreds of sales a week and need the item number in order to identify it). You should be precise about dates. If the seller simply overlooked it, a gentle reminder will spur them into action.

The item was damaged in transit
You need to get back to your seller and gently relay the bad news. If the item was insured it might be covered. In the event of no postal insurance many sellers take responsibility for breakage and will refund money on receipt of a digital picture of the damaged item.

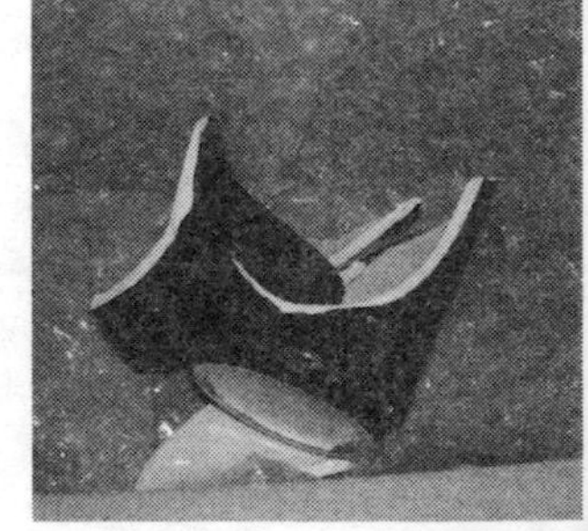

Late one evening you place a winning bid but in the morning you change your mind

A bid is legally binding and you must continue with the purchase. The best way forward is to continue wholeheartedly and promptly with the transaction ensuring that you earn positive feedback. If it fails to grow on you when it arrives you can always sell it on!

The item fails to arrive and the seller does not respond

You need to email, very politely, and point out that you will be forced to take further steps to secure the item or refund. If there is still no response you need to initiate a claim as appropriate. If you paid for the item by a credit card that offers internet cover you should put in a claim. If the item was protected under the PayPal scheme (and paid for using PayPal), you are covered for up to £500. If this does not apply you are covered up to £105 (£120 less £15 administration charge) for Buyer Protection.

The item falls short of the description

You need to take a step back and ensure that your disappointment is not fired by assumptions that you made about the item. If this is not the case, you need to email the seller and very politely explain how the item fails to match up to the description. For example 'you described the item as perfect but there is a chip on the dog's ear'. Such mistakes are easily made and you should ask your seller to suggest a solution. He or she might offer a financial adjustment or refund. Much of the success of the outcome will depend on the tone of your email and, in most cases, with heightened diplomacy the transaction can be successfully completed and positive feedback exchanged.

You have come across an auction of banned items
You should report this to eBay who will investigate it. You can initiate this process in the Help section. You should use the link **Prohibited and Restricted Items.**

Rules and Policies
User Agreement | Prohibited and Restricted Items
Reporting Policy Violations | more...

You feel sure a seller is offering a fake item as genuine
You should report this to eBay who will look into it and if you are proved right they will stop the auction. You can initiate this process by going to **Safety Centre** which is located on the top left-hand side of **Help** pages.

As your auction comes to an end your computer crashes
Go to another computer with an internet connection or even an internet café – providing you have your user ID and password you can access your auctions from anywhere.

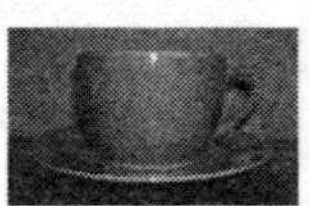

Your credit card will soon expire
You can easily switch or update the credit card that eBay keep on file. Go to **My eBay / Account / Personal Information / Financial Information / Credit Card.** Click on to the **Edit** link on the right-hand side of the page.

You have forgotten your User ID
You can discover your User ID providing that you have your email address.Go to **Site Map / My Account / Forgot Your User ID.** (See next)

You want to place a bid on an item but you have forgotten your password

eBay have a tried and tested route for traders that forget their password. You should go to **Site Map / My Account / Forgot Your Password.**

PayPal Account

Subscriptions

Forgot Your Password

Forgot Your User ID

Your Secret Question

You have discovered a hairline crack on an item you have entered in an auction and described as perfect

You can easily revise details of your auction. Go to the auction page to locate the edit link. If you have received a bid on your auction you should email the bidder, explain the problem and ask if they would like to cancel their bid.

Whilst packing up an item that you described as perfect, and successfully sold, you discover a chip

You should email the buyer straight away and explain the situation. You should ask them if they want to continue with the purchase with some sort of financial adjustment. If you are open and honest about the mistake you may well be able to reach a compromise.

You do not want any more dealings with a particular buyer

It is possible to block particular traders from your auctions. Go to **Site Map / Selling Activities** and select the link **Manage Bidders**. This will take you to the Blocked Buyer List page where you can add or delete names at any time.

Your high and only bidder has pulled out of the transaction

You need to claim back the final value fee by going to **Site Map / Selling / Request Final Value Fee Credit.**

Your buyer has paid with PayPal but forgot to include the cost of shipping.

PayPal offers a very easy means of refunding payment. You should send a friendly note pointing out that he forgot to add the cost of shipping and remind him of the total.

I want my buyers to know that I accept PayPal

Go to **My eBay / My Account / Preferences / Payment from Buyers / Offer PayPal on my listings.**

Payment from buyers	
Use checkout	No
Offer PayPal on my listings	Yes

I am a keen collector of Muffin the Mule items and am afraid that I will miss things that come up for auction.

You can direct eBay to email you whenever a Muffin the Mule item comes up for auction. You can start a search by going to **My eBay / All Favourites / Searches.** Click the link **Add to search** and complete the form.

(Link located on right-hand side.)

16. Explanation of Terms

About Me

This is a page you can create on eBay that gives background about you and your business. It promotes trust and empathy between traders.

Announcement Boards

These are the pages where you will find the latest news and information. You will find details about policy changes, special events and new features and promotions.

Answer Centre

These are pages where eBay members can share knowledge and answer each other's questions.

Auction Style Listing

The auction style listing is the original and basic method of selling on eBay. Auction style listings offer a time span during which interested parties place their bids.

Bid Cancellation

This is the cancellation of a bid by a seller during an auction listing. This is not a common occurrence but there are occasions when a seller, who is not happy about a particular bid, believes that it is necessary.

Bid Retraction

This refers to the withdrawal of a bid by a buyer during an auction listing. Such a course of action is largely frowned upon and special circumstances have to apply before it is allowed.

Bidder Search

You can use a member's User ID to see what items they have placed bids on over the past 30 days.

Buy It Now

This is a feature that allows buyers to purchase an item immediately, for a specified price. To qualify to use this facility sellers must have either a minimum feedback rating of 10 or have signed up for Direct Debit. Buy It Now auctions display the BIN symbol.

Category Listing

Items entered into eBay auctions are allocated a category by the seller.

Changed User ID Icon

Most eBay members like to keep the same User ID as it is part of their trading identity. However, on rare occasions it is necessary to change User ID (the original one might have been too complicated). For 30 days after the change they display a New User ID Icon. A member who has changed their User ID maintains the same profile.

Completed Search

This is a search for items that have sold during the past 15 days. It can be useful for buyers and sellers to see what prices were achieved.

Contact Information

eBay users provide contact information when they register, including name, address and phone number.

Discussion Boards

These are special boards where members can leave messages for the eBay community on a wide range of topics. Experiences are shared and questions answered.

Dutch Auctions

Listings in which sellers offer identical items for sale, for example a seller might offer 50 videos starting at £2. Unlike single item auctions dutch auctions can have many winners as buyers specify how many items they wish to buy.

eBay Pulse

eBay pulse provides an up-to-the-minute report on the up and coming and fastest selling items on eBay. It is of interest to motivated sellers who want to keep up with the latest trends.

eBay Stores

Special pages on eBay offering a range of items that are available for immediate purchase. eBay stores help sellers maximize their business through promotions and displays. Unique items are favoured as eBay offer lower listing costs for items appearing exclusively in their Store.

eBay Time

The time of day at eBay headquarters in the USA.

eBay Toolbar

This is a free eBay buying tool to add to your web browser that allows you to track items that interest you.

Escrow

This is a procedure whereby a third party temporarily holds the buyers money until they signify that they are happy with the item. The money is then sent to the seller, less the escrow agent's fee. This is usually only used for high price transactions

Featured Gallery

This option gives your item a higher profile by featuring it in the special features section above the general Gallery and also appears in larger format within the general Gallery.

Feedback

A system that allows eBay members to rate their buying or selling experience with another trader. See Chapter 4.

Feedback Stars

The stars change colour depending on the level of a member's feedback score.

Final Value Fee

The fee eBay charges the seller when an auction results in a sale.

Fixed Price Format

A selling format whereby the item is offered at a specific price with no bidding involved.

Gallery

A small picture that allows buyers a glimpse of the item.

Gift Services

A listing option that lets you promote the item you are selling as an ideal gift.

ID Verified

This signifies that the checks are complete and the seller's identity has been confirmed.

Insertion Fee

The non-refundable fee charged for submitting an item for auction.

Item Lookup

You can use the item number to find a particular auction.

Merge

Merging accounts is a means of simplifying things for traders with more than one User ID.

Multiple Item Auction

Another expression for a Dutch Auction – see above. To qualify to use this facility, sellers must have a feedback rating of 20 or more and to have been registered on eBay for at least 14 days.

My eBay

This is a bit like your house – everything in My eBay concerns you and only you can go there. It contains your watching, bidding, buying, selling, sold, account details, preferences, etc.

My Messages

This is a security innovation where members receive secure, appropriate messages from eBay and other eBay traders. All messages are guaranteed to be authentic.

New Listing Icon

This indicates that an item has been listed within the last 24 hours.

Outbid

When another buyer has placed a higher bid and you are no longer the high bidder.

PayPal

eBay's preferred online paying facility that allows instant and secure payment.

Power Seller

Indicates a high level of activity and a positive feedback score of at least 98%.

Private Auction

This is a listing in which the User ID of bidders are not displayed to others.

Proxy Bidding

The facility by which a buyer enters the highest sum they would be prepared to pay for an item and eBay automatically bids on their behalf. They only go to the maximum bid if it is required.

Registered Member

A person who has registered with eBay.

Re-listing

Listing an item for sale after it did not sell previously.

Reserve Price

A price that is higher than the start price but below which you would not be prepared to sell. The lowest reserve price permissible is £50. Reserve prices are only known by the seller and are used to protect against bad selling days.

Safety Centre

eBay's range of services designed to keep the eBay Community safe from fraud and poor trading practice.

Second chance offer

This is a feature whereby you can offer the item to a non-winning bidder.

Secure Server

A special Secure Sockets Layer (SSL) encryption server used for processing credit cards and other private information.

Seller Search

A search for a particular seller on eBay.

Selling Manager

An advanced eBay selling tool that allows you carry out your listing and sales-related activities from one location in My eBay.

Shill Bidding

This refers to the illegal placing of bids to artificially raise the price of an item.

Sniping

Placing a bid in the closing minutes or seconds of an auction.

Start Price

This is the opening price for the item in your auction.

Title Search

This is a keyword search for words in the auction title.

Turbo Lister

Turbo lister is a sophisticated eBay selling tool that allows sellers to create multiple listings on their computers offline.

User Agreement

The terms under which eBay offers their services.

User ID

The nickname you select for yourself and by which you are known by other traders.

Want It Now

It is now possible for buyers seeking specific or unusual items to tell sellers what they want. Requests are posted under category headings and available to sellers.

ABBREVIATIONS

NR – No reserve

BNWT – Brand new with tag

BNWOT – Brand new without tag

MIB – Mint in box

N/Mint – Nearly mint condition

NRFB – Never removed from box

MIP – Mint in packet

17. My eBay

home | pay | site map

Buy | Sell | My eBay | Community | Help

On most occasions you will go straight to My eBay when logging onto the site. My eBay keeps track of all of your activities in one convenient spot and, with a click of the mouse it is easy to discover how your auctions and bids are faring. But it contains a great deal more.

My eBay also holds your personal and financial details and is where you come to initiate changes. It also offers a handy link to your **PayPal** account and is where you come to view and initiate **Feedback**. My eBay has been enhanced considerably over the years and now includes **Want It Now** and **My Messages**. This introduction describes some of the most important aspects (but not all) of My eBay to aid beginners.

eBay User ID

cherrypie

Forgot your User ID?

Password

●●●●●●●

Forgot your password?

Sign In Securely >

Having clicked on the **My eBay** link at the top of the home page you will need to give your user ID and password to gain access to the opening page.

This takes you into the opening page of My eBay. You are now set to view, check, update, edit and initiate.

My Summary runs down the left-hand side of the opening page of My eBay and consists of a list of links to pages holding the various activities.

My Summary

All Buying
- Watching (8)
- Bidding (3)
- Best Offers
- Won (7)
- Didn't Win (2)
- My Recommendations

My Summary commences with **All Buying** and lists all buying related activities. In the example on the left the trader is Watching 8 items, Bidding on 3, Won 7 but Didn't Win 2. You can click on any of these links to access the page and survey the details.

PHILOSOPHY - Plato for Beginners

£1.26 £1.80 3 tes

BESWICK FLYING DUCK – 5961 – L

This picture shows two of the 8 items being watched in My eBay.

The Watching page shows a gallery picture of the item (if the seller has provided one), number of bids, current price and ID of the high bidder amongst other things. It also indicates when the auction is due to end.

Watching enables you to keep an eye on an auction without actually placing a bid.

It is possible to remove items from this and any of the other pages by using the delete box at the bottom.

All Selling
- Scheduled (1)
- Selling (2)
- Sold (9)
- Unsold (5)

My eBay holds all your selling related activities in **All Selling**. In the example shown there is 1 Scheduled auction (where the seller has chosen to delay the start of the auction). There are 2 ongoing auctions, 9 Sold items, 5 Unsold items.

Scheduled auctions are created when items are listed – using the Sell link at the top of the home page. There are many reasons that sellers elect to delay the start of an auction but often concerned with the time it ends.

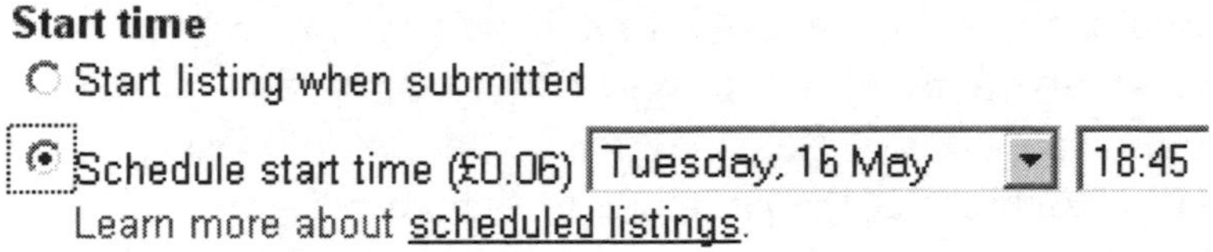

Start time

○ Start listing when submitted

◉ Schedule start time (£0.06) Tuesday, 16 May 18:45

Learn more about scheduled listings.

Selling

Selling is one of the most practical links in My eBay allowing you to view your active auctions in one place. You can track the bids and watchers as your auction progresses. As many buyers do not bid until the end of the auction, watchers is a useful indication of interest.

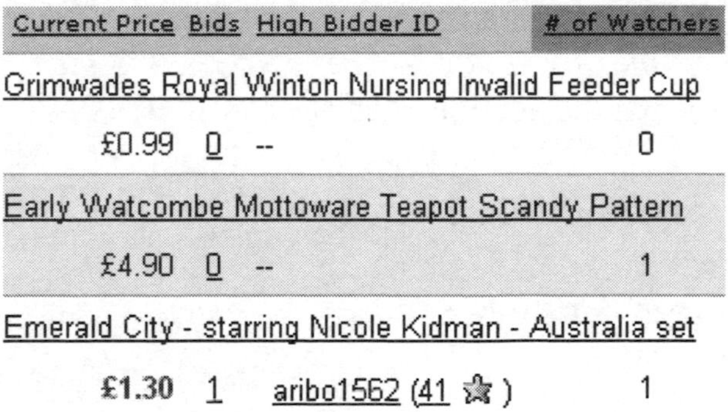

Current Price	Bids	High Bidder ID	# of Watchers
Grimwades Royal Winton Nursing Invalid Feeder Cup			
£0.99	0	--	0
Early Watcombe Mottoware Teapot Scandy Pattern			
£4.90	0	--	1
Emerald City - starring Nicole Kidman - Australia set			
£1.30	1	aribo1562 (41 ☆)	1

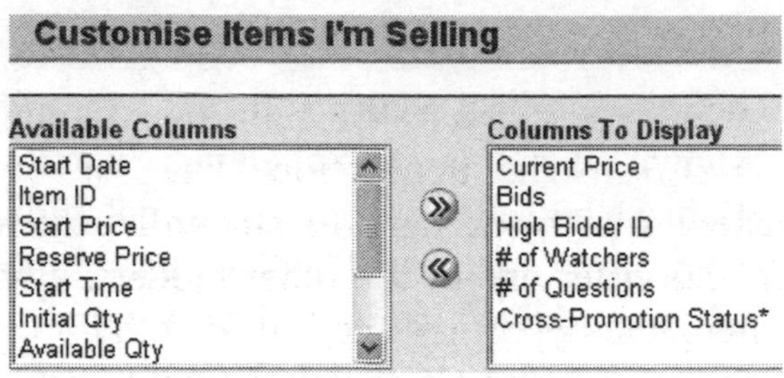

You can choose the information that is displayed on the Selling page. Click on the **Customise** link on the top right.

Sold – When you have successfully sold an item you should come to the Sold link in My eBay to send your buyer an invoice and progress the transaction. You will find a reminder of the final price and cost of postage. You will also discover the postcode of the winner.

On the far right of this page is a chart that tracks the progress of sales, showing when an item has been paid for, sent and feedback posted and received.

Second Chance Offer

It occasionally happens that a high bidder fails to pay for an item and withdraws from the transaction. This is very frustrating for sellers who work hard to streamline their operations. Sellers can offer one of the other bidders, who failed to win the item, the opportunity to buy it at the price of their bid. This Second Chance Offer link is found via the Bid History link in the completed auction.

ıs291999 (9) Send Second Chance Offer	£120.00	07-May-06 14:4(
ırdingsofsway (35 ☆) Send Second Chance Offer	£102.50	07-May-06 11:0
ıs291999 (9) Send Second Chance Offer	£99.99	07-May-06 14:4(
ıs291999 (9) Send Second Chance Offer	£92.97	07-May-06 14:4(

Unsold – Similarly, you can view unsold items where you will find a convenient Re-list link. It is an opportunity to re-think the strategy and try again.

Item ID	High Bid	Bids	# of Watchers
Grimwades Royal Winton Nursing Invalid Feeder Cup			
6278228876	--	0	0
Emerald City - starring Nicole Kidman - Australia set			
9134252252	--	0	0

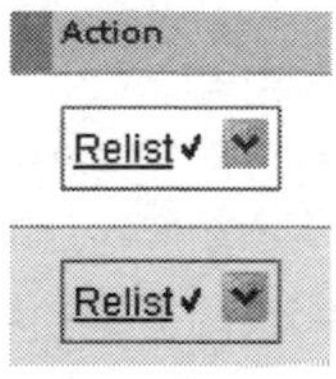

It is important to get things right second time around because when a re-listed item sells eBay refunds the listing fee.

Want It Now NEW!

Want It Now is an enhancement requested by users to aid both buyers and sellers.

Buyers

Create a Want It Now post and tell millions of sellers what you want.

Post To Want It Now

It's Free

Tip: You can view all your posts in My eBay

Buyers seeking something rare or unusual can post a request on the site. As with selling they must write a title and description of what they are seeking and place it in a category. It is recommended that buyers are as specific as possible.

Browse Want It Now

Antiques & Art
Automotive
Baby
Books, Comics & Magazines
Business, Office & Industrial
Clothes, Shoes & Accessories
Coins
Collectables

Sellers who are keen and pro-active can browse through the Want It Now postings to discover the things that have a ready market. If they have a requested item they can list it, alternatively they can keep an eye out for it.

My Messages (7)

Another extremely useful innovation to My eBay has been the introduction of **My Messages**. This section provides a boost to the security of the site concerning fake emails. An ongoing problem for honest traders has been the prevalence of fraudulent emails claiming to be from eBay. The emails are an attempt to get hold of the IDs and passwords of established members so that they can be used to dupe other traders. It has been difficult to stop these emails as they are so convincing that occasionally members have been fooled. eBay have overcome this problem by setting up **My Messages**.

My Messages
I have 7 new messages.

All bona fide communication, whether it is from eBay or eBay members, is duplicated in **My Messages**. When you receive an email that appears to be from eBay you should go straight to My Messages to see if it is there. You can access the message by clicking on the title.

☐	Flag	From	Subject
☐		eBay	List your item for just 5p
☐		9hshell	Re: Message from eBay Member Regarding Item #7411287144

When you have read the message you can delete it using the box to the left of the page and clicking **Delete**.

All Favourites
- Searches
- Sellers
- Categories

Further down the list of links comes **All Favourites**. This enables you to store specific searches so that you are alerted by email when they come up.

Name of Search	Search Criteria
flying Beswick duck	**flying Beswick duck** Sort: Ending First
midwinter dog	**midwinter dog** Sort: Ending First

Searches - The above example illustrates two saved searches. This means that each time an item is listed with 'flying Beswick duck' or 'Midwinter dog' in the title, an email will be sent by eBay. It saves collectors and buyers the trouble of scouring eBay for the items they desire.

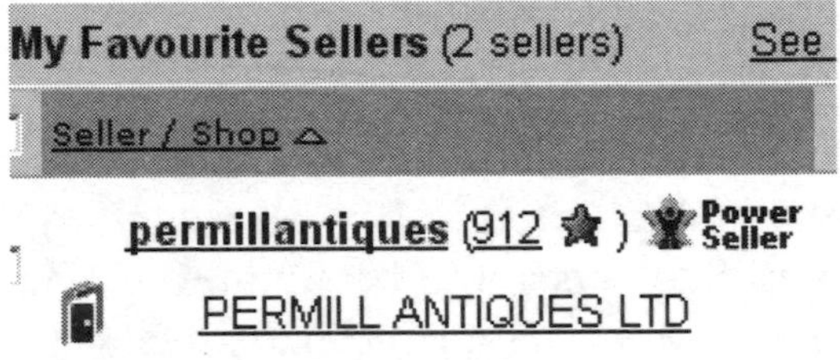

Sellers - Similarly it is possible to save searches for sellers so that you are informed when new items are listed by this particular trader.

Categories - Category searches can also be saved for buyers seeking particular types of goods. For example collectors of early wine bottles might want to save the search:

Collectables / Bottles & Pots / Wine

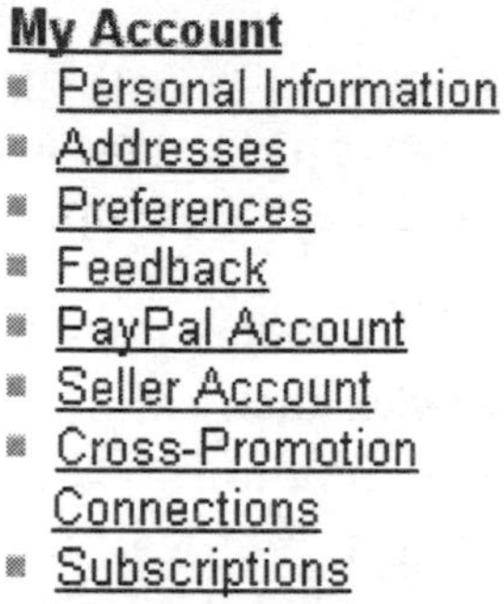

My Account
- Personal Information
- Addresses
- Preferences
- Feedback
- PayPal Account
- Seller Account
- Cross-Promotion Connections
- Subscriptions

If **My eBay** is considered as your 'house' on the site, **My Account** corresponds to your 'study' in your house as it contains all the administrative 'paperwork'. This is where you will come to make changes to the details that eBay hold about you and your account, such as your address.

Every page offers an easy link to make the required changes. Some are concerned with keeping details current whilst others, such as **Selling Preferences,** allow members to customize the site to their exact requirements.

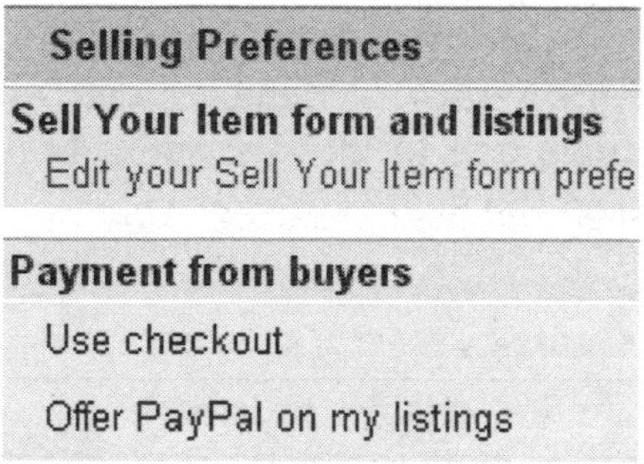

Selling Preferences

Sell Your Item form and listings

Edit your Sell Your Item form prefe

Payment from buyers

Use checkout

Offer PayPal on my listings

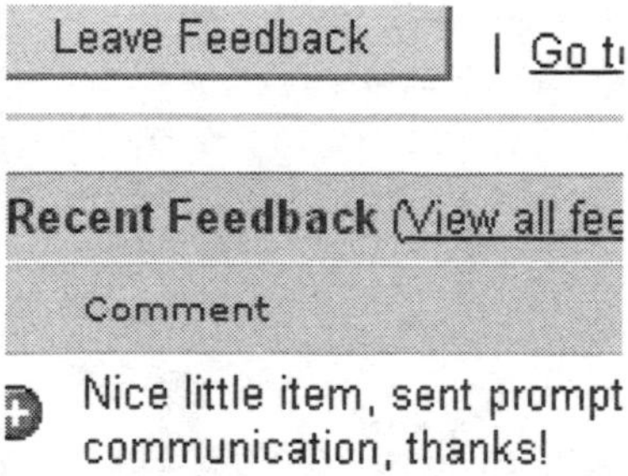

Leave Feedback | Go t

Recent Feedback (View all fee

Comment

Nice little item, sent prompt communication, thanks!

The **Feedback** link is another that you will use frequently. It offers a straightforward means of reading the latest feedback comments left about you, and for leaving your feedback for other traders.

PayPal – Although PayPal is separate from eBay there is a seamless link to assist its use.

My Reviews & Guides

There is much emphasis on the community side of eBay and Reviews and Guides capture the spirit of it.

Reviews offers a forum where traders can share their opinions about products. You can read reviews left by others or write your own.

Top Review - Members can vote on the reviews that are submitted to the page and the winners are highlighted in Top Review.

Guides

Guides enable members to share their knowledge on any topic. If you have particular expertise that you think other members will find useful, you should get cracking.

- How to Plan the Perfect Holiday
- The Essential DVD Collection
- All About Podcasts & Podcasting

As with the reviews, members are invited to vote for the most useful guides which may appear on the Reviews & Guides Home Page.

18. Fast Track Summary

Your user ID and password are required for the following:

Create Your Auction

Home Page

Sell Link

Select selling format (online auction or fixed price)

Select **Sell Your Item**

Check Your Auction

Home Page

My eBay

My Summary, All Selling, **Selling**

Change Description of Item in Current Auction

Home Page

My eBay

My Summary, All Selling, **Selling**

Enter auction by clicking on title

Click **Revise your item**

Click **Edit title & description**

Make changes

Save Changes

Contact your High Bidder

Home Page

My eBay

My Summary, All Selling, **Selling**

Enter auction by clicking on title

Click on **bid** in History

Click on first (highest) bid

Click on **Contact member**

Type in message

Click **Send message**

Re-List Item

Home Page

My eBay

My Summary, All Selling, **Unsold**

Locate the completed auction

Click on **Relist**

Make changes using Edit links

Save changes

Submit listing

End Auction Early

Home page

Site Map

Selling Activities

End your listing early

Cancel Bids

Home Page

Site Map

Selling Activities

Click on **Cancel bids on my items**

You need:

- Item number
- User ID of the bidder
- Explanation of less than 80 characters

Click **Cancel bid**

To Send Buyer an Invoice

Home Page

My eBay

My Summary, All Selling, **Sold**

Click **Send buyer an invoice**

Look Up eBay Fees

Home Page

Site Map

Help, **Selling**

Click on **What are eBay's fees?**

Check Your eBay Account
Home Page
My eBay
My Summary, My Account, Seller Account
Click **View Account Status**

To Contact eBay Customer Services
Home Page
Site Map
Help, click on **How do I contact customer support?**

Leave Feedback
Home Page
My eBay
My Summary, My Account, **Feedback**

Check your Feedback
Home Page
My eBay
My Summary, My Account, **Feedback**

Change Your Password
Home Page
My eBay
My Summary, My Account, **Personal Information**
Click **Edit** for password in **Personal Information**

Change Your Credit Card
Home Page
My eBay
My Summary, My Account, **Personal Information**
Click **change** for credit card in **Financial Information**

Change Your Preferences
Home Page
My eBay
My Summary, My Account, **Preferences**
Click **Edit** as appropriate

To Request a Final Value Fee Credit
Home Page
Site Map
Selling
Request final value fee credit

To Retract a Bid with Wrongly Placed Decimal Point
Home Page
Site Map
Buying Resources, **Bid Retractions**
You will need the item number of the auction

Concerning PayPal

Look Up PayPal Fees

Home Page

My eBay

My Summary, My Account, **PayPal Account**

My PayPal Account Information, **Go to My Account**

Click **Fees** link at bottom of page

Go to PayPal Account

Home Page

My eBay

My Summary, My Account, **PayPal Account**

Go to My Account Overview

Transfer Money from PayPal Account

www.paypal.co.uk

Log in using email address and password

Click **Withdraw** link

Select **Transfer funds to your bank account**

Enter amount

Click **Continue**

Organising Pictures on Your Computer

Create a Picture Folder

My Pictures

Right-click to bring up menu

Highlight **New**

Select **Folder**

Type in name and press enter

To Name or Re-name Picture

Highlight picture

Select **File** from toolbar (top of window) to bring up menu

Select **rename**

Press backspace key

Type in name and press enter

To Move Picture of Sold Item to Sold Folder

My Pictures

Open folder containing picture

Select picture of item sold

Click on **Edit** to bring up menu

Select **Move to Folder** to bring up list of folders

Highlight **eBay Sold** folder in **My Pictures**

Click **Move**

18 Fast Track Summary

Index